Maharshi Dayanand Saraswati Book Series-29

Śri Śankarāchārya's

Aparokṣānubhuti

Direct Realization

Prof. Ravi Prakash Arya
Chair Professor
Maharshi Dayanand Saraswati Chair (UGC)
Maharshi Dayanand University, Haryana

Amazon Books, USA
In Association with
Indian Foundation for Vedic Science
H.O.1051, Sector-1, Rohtak, Haryana, India
Ph. 9313033917; 9650183260
Email: vedicscience@rediffmail.com; vedicscience@gmail.com
https://vedic-sciences.com

First Edition
Kali Era 5127 (Christian era 2025)
Kalpa Era 1,972,949, 127
Brahma Era 155,521,972,949,127

ISBN: 978-93-94724-98-3

Printed by
Indian Foundation for Vedic Science, 1051, Sector-1, Rohtak-124001, Haryana.

Contents

Preface

Aprokṣānubhūti, as its name implies, delves into the methods of achieving direct self-realization and Brahma-realization, bypassing the conventional indirect methods and means. The concept of 'Direct Self-Realization' and 'Brahma Realization' eliminates the idea of worship of any physical form, including human bodies or material objects like mūrtis. A seeker aspiring for direct self-realization and Brahma-realization must renounce the worship of any Devas, such as Krishna, Shiva, Vishnu, Hanumāna, or any Devīs, like Durgā, Kāli, or Pārvatī, and others. Continuation of the above practice hinders the attainment of self-realization. The first prerequisite for self-realization is to refrain from mistaking even one's own body for a soul. Mistaking other bodies (third party) for souls is futile in achieving the goal of mokṣa. In the second stage, the seeker must transcend the existence of their body and recognize their true nature as the reality independent of the physical form. They should not feel dependent on their body. They need not seek worship of Rāma, Krishna, Durga, Kali, or any other deity; instead, they should recognize their inherent potential to become like these, as everyone possesses this capacity. When this profound understanding and realization are achieved, the seeker will experience the joy of their self-existence distinct from the body, mind, or senses. Brahma-realization takes place when soul forgets its own existence and become one with Brahman. This called mokṣa. In the fourth stage, it is crucial to understand that the primary obstacles to self-realization and Brahma-realization are known as upādhis in philosophical terminology. Upādhi refers to a separating wall that creates a barrier between the soul and

Brahman. For instance, a room has its own space, and the walls separate it from the universal space. These walls function as upādhis, dividing the room's space from the universal space. When these separator walls are demolished, the room's space merges with the universal space. Conversely, when the walls are rebuilt, the room's space separates from the universal space. In the case of a room, the walls are either demolished or constructed by its owner.

Similarly, the soul accompanies the subtle body, which consists of mana, chitta, buddhi, and ahaṅkāra. These are permanently attached to the soul and act as upādhi (separator) between the soul and Brahman. For the soul to attain mokṣa, these upādhis must not be deactivated; they should remain inactive. Now, the question arises: how does this upādhi activates, and how to keep it deactivated?

The chitta is activated when sanskāras (information) of the material world are accumulated in the mind. This information (sanskāra) helps activate an upādhi of the body for the soul, and the soul identifies itself with this upādhi (material body) which is the second party (dvaita), persistence of this phenomenon is called as embodiment or bondage of the soul.

At the first level, if a soul desiring mokṣa must deactivate the upādhi (body) by withdrawing its attention from the material world so that further information or sanskāra from the outside world is not accumulated, the second upādhi is ahaṅkāra (sense of individuality). Ahaṅkāra is like the wall that separates the soul from Brahman. If the soul continues to enjoy the notion of ahaṅkāra, it cannot attain mokṣa even when it has emptied its mind of the information of the material world. How is this possible?

Firstly, neglect or negate the body to deactivate it and feel that you are separate from the body. This is called sef-realization. The term mithyā defines this negation or neglection of the body which is ever-changing and useless for mokṣa. Secondly, when a person continues to meditate upon Brahman and completely surrenders to Him, his wall of ahaṅkāra is also deactivated, and they attain mokṣa.

Therefore, the message of Advaita is very clear. You are a unique entity and develop yourself to the level of gods and goddesses. Do not engage in their worship or any worship of human forms or objects. Do not concentrate on the tip of your nose. Feel the Brahman's presence everywhere and realize your true identity that you are immaterial element independent of the body.

ब्रह्म सत्यं जगन्मिथ्या (*Brahma satyaṁ jaganmithyā*) translates to "Brahman is eternal, while the world in motion is perishable." It is crucial to recognize that there are two distinct types of worlds: the visible world, which is perpetually in motion called jagat or sansāra, and the invisible world (prakṛti or inactive energy/dark energy), which remains stationary. Consequently, the invisible world or prakṛti or dark energy is also eternal.

The authorship of "Aprokṣānubhūti" is frequently attributed to Śri Ādi Śaṅkarāchārya. However, a preliminary examination of the Sanskrit verses suggests that this text may not have been penned by him, as the quality of some verses is noticeably subpar. The similies employed by the author in several instances lack the standard one would expect in a philosophical treatise of this caliber. Thus, it appears that this brief work was composed by a Neo-Vedāntin under the name of

Śaṅkarāchārya.

Ādi Śaṅkara was a self-realized soul, a great scholar and a profound yogī following the Mahābhārata war. His doctrine of Advaita has not been fully grasped by Neo-Vedāntins. According to Śaṅkara, the concept of Advaita applies at the Pārmārthika level (mokṣa) rather than at the Vyavahārika level. He taught that this world is ever-changing, which is why he described it as mithyā (impermanent). Consequently, meditation on transient objects cannot lead to mokṣa. If one worships any material form or object, they cannot realize Brahman, the ultimate reality.

As a result, Śaṅkarāchārya opposed the veneration of material forms, such as mūrtis. The practice of Mūrtipūjā originated with Buddhists, was adopted by Jains, and later embraced by Sanātanīs. In his commentary on the *Śrimad Bhagavad Gītā* (18.21), Śri Krishna states that considering a human being as God and engaging in idolatry or Mūrtipūjā are forms of tāmasika worship. Typically, idolaters or worshippers of human forms confine God to a specific idol or human form they revere, failing to recognize the divinity that transcends these representations.

In this context, Śaṅkara himself critiques mūrtipūjā in his commentary while referring to the Buddhists. For example, he notes:

एकस्मिन् कार्ये (देहे बहिः वा प्रतिमादौ) सक्तम् (एतावान् एव आत्मा ईश्वरो वा न अतः परम् अस्ति इति यथा नग्नक्षपणकादीनां शरीरानुवर्ती देहपरिमाणो जीव ईश्वरो वा पाषाणदार्वामात्र इति एवम् एकस्मिन् कार्ये सक्तम्)।

ēkasmin kārye (dehe bahiḥ vā pratimādau) saktam (ētāvān ēva ātmā īśvaro vā na ataḥ param asti iti yathā nagnakṣapaṇakādīnāṁ śarīrānuvartī dehaparimāṇo jīva īśvaro vā pāṣāṇadārvāmātra iti ēvam ēkasmin kārye saktam).

[Meaning] Delimiting All-pervading Brahman into one single effect means delimiting Him into a body or some (*pratimā*) mūrti. Only this human form or mūrti is Brahman or Īśvara and nothing is beyond it. Just as Digambara Jains consider the measurement of Īśvara or ātmā equal to the human body or idolators think that Brahman is limited to a particular mūrti made up of stone or wood.

This viewpoint fundamentally challenges the worship of material objects or forms. In contrast, Neo-Vedāntins embrace Mūrtipūjā, mistakenly holding that an inert mūrti made of matter can embody the divine. This misconception is as misguided as equating the body with the soul itself. In this treatise, we strive to unveil the true essence of Śaṅkara's Advaita philosophy, encouraging a deeper understanding of the divine that transcends mere physical representations.

The Epoch of Ādi Śaṅkarāchārya

1168 BC-1136 BC

The epoch of Ādi Śaṅkarāchārya holds significant importance in Indian history, yet there is considerable debate surrounding its precise date. Four maṭhas established by Śaṅkarāchārya failed to maintain a consistent chronological record of Śaṅkarāchārya's tenure as the head of the maṭhas. It appears that they commenced recording events five to six centuries after the establishment of their respective maṭhas.

Deciphering the actual date of Śaṅkarāchārya holds the potential to resolve numerous riddles pertaining to the chronology of Indian history. Despite the clear-cut records of Śaṅkara's date in Sanskrit literature, it remains a subject of scholarly and historical contention due to the limited understanding of Indian eras.

In this analysis, we will consider accounts from various texts that provide dates attributed to Śaṅkarāchārya. However, we will refrain from examining records of Maṭhas founded by Śaṅkara, as these records are unreliable and poorly maintained. Furthermore, every pontiff who assumed the headship of Maṭhas has been known as Śaṅkarāchārya. All of these Śaṅkarāchāryas dedicated their lives to the propagation of dharma. Consequently, the various dates provided by historians are associated with any one of these Śaṅkarāchāryas. It is not necessary that all of these dates pertain to the initial Śaṅkarāchārya who established the Maṭhas for the safeguarding of dharma. The use of multiple names can be confusing and hinder the attainment of accurate conclusions.

In this study, we will focus on the case of the first

Śaṅkara who established the four Maṭhas.

First View

The most compelling evidence is provided by a book titled "Bāla Maṅkha Śekhara," which is quoted by Thakur Nagina Ram Parmar in his renowned work "Tvārīkha-e-Kadim Āryāvartta," published in Urdu in 1887. According to him, this book states that in the Tiṣya or Tikha Saṁvat 3889, when vibhava Saṁvat was in currency, Śaṅkarāchārya was born in the auspicious Muhurta within the house of Śivaguru. As previously mentioned, Tikha Saṁvat became prevalent 1955 years prior to Kaliyuga. It remained in currency until the time of Emperor Yudhiṣṭhira.

Comparing this information with our table, we find that Tikha Saṁvat 3889 corresponds to the 1934 Kali era, the 2006 Yudhiṣṭhira era, and 1168 BC. Additionally, our "9000 Years Calendar of Various Indian Eras" confirms that during that period, Vibhava Saṁvatsara of the Daivi (Northern) tradition was in currency. Therefore, based on this evidence, it is concluded that the first Śaṅkarāchārya or Ādi Śaṅkara was born in 1168 BC.

1. The aforementioned assertion is substantiated by the statement contained in the renowned Semi Puranic text titled 'Śiva Rahaṣya' (Aṁśa 9. Ch. 8. Stanza 16). Consequently, Śaṅkara was born prior to the conclusion of the second millennium of Kaliyuga. The Sanskrit text is as follows:

कल्यादिमे महादेवि सहस्रद्वितीयादपरम ॥

[Meaning] Śaṅkara was born prior to the 2nd Millenium of Kaliyuga.

The above date of 1168 BC corresponds to Kaliyuga

year 1934 which stands prior to the end of 2nd Millenium of the Kaliyuga.

Tradition holds that Patañjali instructed Gaudapada, who in turn taught Govindapada, the Guru of Śaṅkara. Consequently, Patañjali and Śaṅkara must have been separated by a maximum of 100 years. Patañjali's date of birth has been determined to be 1200 BC. Therefore, the date above Śivarahasya appears to be accurate.

2. Currently, I may adopt the prevailing historical perspective, which posits that Śaṅkara resided from AD 788 to AD 820. K.B. Pathak has supported this view based on a three-page manuscript he discovered in Belgaum. The manuscript's colophon reveals that the individual who bestows salvation directly incarnated as Śaṅkarāchārya on Earth to combat evil conduct. The emergence of Śaṅkara transpired in the year known as Vibhava during the Tikha SaŠvat 3889. At the tender age of eight, he immersed himself in the study of the four Vedas; at twelve, he composed all the Śāstras assigned to him; at sixteen, he authored the renowned commentary; and at thirty-two, the sage departed. In the Kaliyuga, the year 3921, Tikha Saṁvat witnessed his entry into the cave. On the full moon day of Vaiśākha, Śaṅkara attained the sacred status of 'Śivahood'. The Sanskrit text elucidates this event as follows:

दुष्टाचार-विनाशाय प्रादुर्भूतो महीतले ।

स एव शंकराचार्य साक्षात्कैवल्यनायकः ॥

निधिनागेभवह्न्याब्दे (3889) विभवे शंकरः ।

अष्टवर्षे चतुर्वेदी द्वादशे सर्वशास्त्रकृत् ।

षोडशे कृत्वान् भाष्यं द्वत्रिंशे मुनिरभ्यगात् ॥

कल्यब्दे चन्द्रनेत्रांक वह्न्यब्दे (3921) गुहाप्रवेशः ।

वैशाखे पूर्णिमायां तु शंकरः शिवतामियात् ॥

duṣṭāchāra-vināśāya prādurbhūto mahītale /
sa ēva śaṁkarāchārya sākṣātkaivalyanāyakaḥ //
nidhināgebhavahnyābde (3889) vibhave śaṁkaraḥ /
aṣṭavarṣe chaturvedī dvādaśe sarvaśāstrakṛt /
ṣoḍaśe kṛtvān bhāṣyaṁ dvatriṁśe munirabhyagāt //
kalyabde chandranetrāṁka vahnyabde (3921) guhāpraveśaḥ /
vaiśākhe pūrṇimāyāṁ tu śaṁkaraḥ śivatāmiyāt //

The above reference of Manuscript discovered by K.B. Pathak is nothing but the repetition of the statement of the text of 'Bāla Maṅkha Śekhara' quoted in para no. 1 above. This manuscript was composed based upon the statement of 'Bāla Maṅkha Śekhara'. Here the year 3889 does not refer to Kali year but Tiṣya or Tikha year as quoted by Thakur Nagina Ram Parmar. In the sixth stanza, the word 'abda' has been repeated with 'kali' and 'vahni' which means 'in Kaliyuga' and Tiṣya Saṁvatsar. So the above reference supports the view that Śaṅkara was born after a lapse of 3889 years of Tiṣya Saṁvat, in 1934 Kali, or 1168 BC, in Vibhava Saṁvatsara of Jupiter according to the Daivi or Northern tradition. Here it may also be pointed out that 788 ADalso corresponds to 'Vibhava' Saṁvatsara of Āsuri tradition. But it does not tally with other references. The above Śloka also informs that Śaṅkara died after 3921 (expired) Tiṣya Saṁvat, i.e. 1966 Kali, or 8th April 1136 BC on Vaiśākha Pūrṇimā, Saturday. The details are as under:

30 April 1136 BC, Sunday	Chaitra Amāvasyā
2 May 1136 BC, Tuesday	Sun ingresses in Vṛṣabha
12th May 1136 BC, Tuesday	Vaiśākha S-11

16th May 1136 BC, Tuesday   Vaiśākha Pūrṇimā

30th May 1136 BC, Tuesday   Vaiśākha Amāvasyā

3. Some other works may also be quoted to support the above view. They are Nilakantha Bhatta's 'Śaṅkara Mandāra Saurabha' and 'Śaṅkarābhyudaya'. According to these texts, when 3889 years of Tiṣya Saṁvat elapsed in Kaliyuga, Śaṅkara took birth in Vibhava Saṁvatsar.

नवाधिकाशीति युताष्टशक्त्या युक्ते सहस्रत्रितये (3889) व्यतीते।
तिष्ये समानां विभवाब्दराधासिते दशम्यामुद्भूत महेशः ॥

[Meaning] After the lapse of 3889 years of Tiṣya Saṁvat, Śaṅkara was born in Vibhava year of Jupiter on 10th lunation of Śukla Pakṣa.

Similarly, Krishna Brahmananda's Śaṅkaravijaya also agrees that after the lapse of 3889 years of Tiṣya Saṁvat, Śaṅkara was born. The date was April 28th, 1168 BC, Sunday, the 10th and 11th Lunation of the bright half of the Vaiśākha month. I quote the original Sanskrit texts as under:

निधिनागेभ वह्न्याब्दे (3889) विभवे शंकरोदयः।
तिष्ये तु शालिवाहस्य सखेन्दु शत सप्तके॥

[Meaning] After the lapse of 3889 years of Tiṣya Saṁvat in Vibhava Saṁvatsar Śaṅkara was born.

Here it may be noted that all the above-cited references are quoting Tiṣya Saṁvatsara in Kaliyuga. The precision of these dates and their general agreement gives credence to this view. As such according to the above quoted five views Śaṅkara was born to Śivaguru and Mahādevī in 1168 BC during the currency of Vibhava Saṁvatsara, according to the Daivi or Northern traditionand died in 1136 BC. All these views mention Tiṣya Saṁvat in the 'Kaliyuga' and not Kali era. So we should not confuse Kali era with Tiṣya era. Due to the same obsession and preconceived notion, many historians and Indologists are sticking to the date of 788 AD which is also Vibhava Saṁvatsara.

Second View

The second view is supported by Jain literature. Accordingly, Śaṅkara was born after 2125 Jain Yudhiṣṭhira Saṁvat or 3294-2125= 1169 (expired), i.e.1168 BC and died after 2157 Jain Yudhiṣṭhira Saṁvat or 3294-2157=1137 (expired), i.e. 1136 BC. Yudhiṣṭhira Saṁvat of Jina Vijaya is 3294 BC. Śaṅkara of Jina Vijaya was born in Jupiter year Nandana and died in Jupiter year Tāmrākṣa (Raktākṣa). Referring to the death of Śaṅkara, Jina Vijaya says:

ऋषिर्बाणस्तथा भूमिमर्त्याक्ष (2157) वाममेलनात् ।
एकत्वेन लभेतांकं ताम्राक्षा तत्र वत्सरः ॥

[Meaning] When we calculate the figures ṛṣi=7, bāṇa=5, bhūmi=1 and martyākṣi=2 in the reverse order (2157) and reckon the years in Yudhiṣṭhira Saṁvat after Mahābhārata war we arrive at the year Tāmrākṣa (Raktākṣa) of Jupiter as the year of Śaṅkara's death.

We find that according to the first tradition as cited above, Śaṅkara was born in Vibhava Saṁvatsara and according to the second tradition, Śaṅkara was born in Nandana Saṁvatsara. This difference of Jovial years is in fact due to the difference in traditions. 1168 BC corresponds to Jovial year 'Vibhava' according to 'Daivi' tradition and 'Nandana' according to 'Āsuri' tradition. It was both Vibhava and Nandana Saṁvatsaras in 1168 BC according to Daivi (North Indian) and Āsuri (South Indian) traditions. Our '9000-Years' Calendar of Saptarṣi and other Indian Eras' also clarifies this confusion. So both the views support the same epoch.

Third View

The third view is advocated by various Sanskrit works written in the eulogy of Ādi Śaṅkarācharya. These works include Śaṅkarābhyudaya, Bṛhat Śaṅkara Vijaya, Prāchīna Vijaya and Puṇya Śloka Mañjari etc. All these works have been written after Jain works. Authors of all these works have followed the statement of Jain sources and accepted with one voice that Śaṅkara was born in Nandana Saṁvatsara and died at the age of 32 in Raktākṣī Saṁvatsara. However, they seem to be confused regarding the Tiṣya Saṁvat followed by them, as they are not united and have made statements as per their convenience with a central idea of Nandana Savatsara. For instance, I quote all of them here one by one. According to Prāchīna Vijaya,

तिष्ये प्रयात्यनल(3)-शेवधि (9)-बाण (5)-नेत्रे (2)
अब्दे नंदने दिनमणावुदग्भाजि ॥
राधेऽसितेरुडुविनिर्गतमंगलग्नेऽस्याहूतवान् ।
शिवः शिवगुरुः स च शंकरेति ॥

tiṣye prayātyanala(3)-śevadhi (9)-bāṇa (5)-netre (2)
abde naṁdane dinamaṇāvudagbhāji ॥
rādhe'siteruḍuvinirgatamaṁgalagne'syāhūtavān ।
śivaḥ śivaguruḥ sa cha śaṁkareti ॥

Śaṅkara was born in the year Nandana when 2593 years of Tiṣya era had elapsed.

Prāchina Vijaya quotes first Tiṣya Yudhiṣṭhira era started by Jain in the memory of their Tirthaṅkara.So 2593 years of elapsed Tiṣya Samvat means 3762-2593= 1169, i.e 1168 BC. Thus the date of Śaṅkara, according to Prāchina Vijaya can be fixed as 1169 (expired), i.e. 1168 BC.

Puṇya Śloka Mañjarī quotes the emancipation period of Śaṅkara as 2625. Śaṅkara lived for 32 years, as such his date of birth, according to Puṇya Śloka Mañjarī is 2625-32= 2593 which is almost the same as quoted by Prāchina Vijaya. According to this text, Śaṅkara's Nirvāṇa tithi is Śukla Ekādaśī (12th May 1136 BC). According to others, it was Vaiśākha Pūrṇimā (16th May 1136 BC). So there is confusion among the scholars about the tithi of Śaṅkara's birth and death, that is why differing views are expressed by different scholars. According to one view, Śaṅkara was born on the 11th lunar day of the bright fortnight of Vaiśākha.

महेशांशाज्जातो मधुरमुपदिष्टाद्वय-नयो महामोह।
ध्वान्तप्रशमनरविः षण्मत-गुरुः ।

maheśāṁśājjāto madhuramupadiṣṭādvaya-nayo mahāmoha /
dhvāntapraśamanaraviḥ ṣaṇmata-guruḥ /

फले (32) स्वस्मिन् स्वायुष्यपि शरचराब्देऽपि (2625)।
च कलेः विलल्ये रक्ताषिण्यधिवृष सितैकादशी परे॥
phale (32) svasmin svāyuṣyapi śaracharābde'pi (2625) /
cha kaleḥ vilalye raktāṣiṇyadhivṛṣa sitaikādaśī pare //

The above date corresponds to May 1168 BC, Tuesday.

Bṛhat Śaṅkara Vijaya of Chitsukhāchārya states that Śaṅkara was born in the 31styear when 26 centuries of the Yudhiṣṭhira era had elapsed. It was the Jupiter year Nandana, the month of Vaiśākha (Chaitra), the 5th lunar day of the bright fortnight and a Sunday. The Lagna (ascendant) was Karka and nakṣatra was Punarvasu. This corresponds to 31st March 1168 BC, Sunday. Hereunder I give the horoscope for 31st March 1168 BC. prepared with the help of Astrodienst for the benefit of our readers.

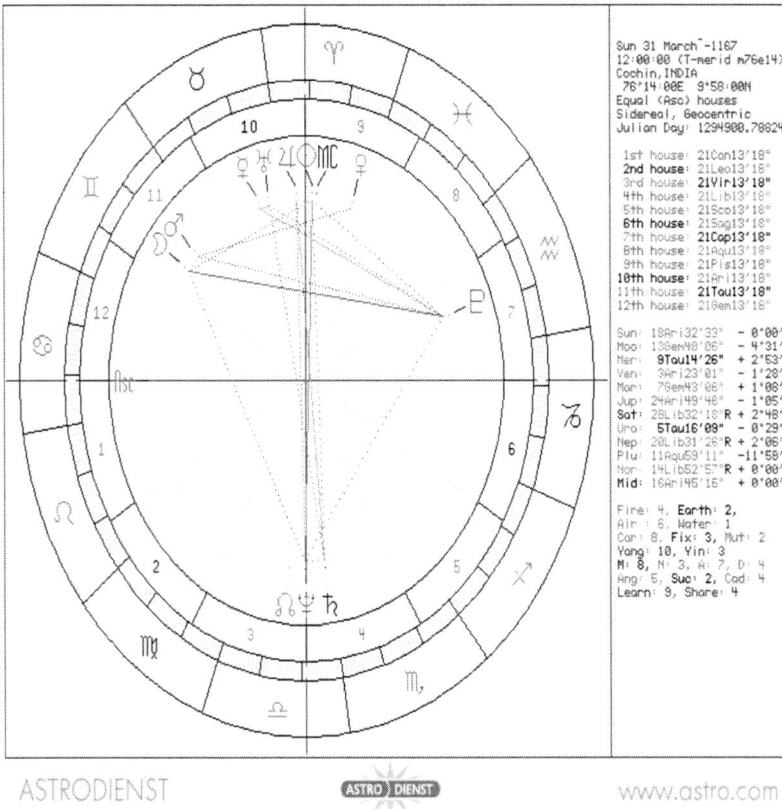

The verse of Bṛhat Śaṅkara Vijaya reads like this:

ततः सा दशमे मासे संपूर्ण शुभलक्षणे ।
षड्विंशे शतके श्रीमद् युधिष्ठिरशकस्य वै ॥
एकत्रिंशेऽथ वर्षे तु हायने नंदने शुभे ।
मेषराशौ गते सूर्येवैशाखे (चैत्रे) मासि शोभने ॥
शुक्लपक्षे च पंचम्यां तिथ्यां भास्करवासरे ।
पुनर्वसु गते चन्द्रे लग्ने कर्कटावह्ये ॥

Calculations for both the dates are as under:

25th Feb. 1168 BC	Phālguna Amāvasyā, Monday
31st March1168 BC	Chaitra S-5, Sunday
1st April 1168 BC	Chaitra S-10, Monday

11th March 1168 BC   Chaitra Pūrṇimā, Monday

25th April 1168 BC   Chaitra Amāvasyā, Wednesday

First of all, let me say that the authenticity of the above śloka is doubtful, because there are several metrical and astronomical errors in it. According to the śloka, the sun was in Meṣa rāśī and the month was Vaiśākha. It is a contrary statement. When the sun is in the Meṣa Saṅkrānti between two Amāvasyās, the month is known as Chaitra. The The Vaiśākha month occurred when the sun is in the Vṛṣabha rāśī. So, the first technical correction required is to say Chaitra month instead of Vaiśākha. Despite this, it appears that the writer of this śloka in the Bṛhat Śaṅkara Vijaya also quotes the first Jain Yudhiṣṭhira Śaka 3762 BC. The exact date of Śaṅkara may be derived, applying his calculations, by adding 36 years of Yudhṣṭhira's rule before or after the war to the first Yudhiṣṭhira Jain Śaka. Accordingly, Śaṅkara was born after a lapse of 2630 years of the first Yudhiṣṭhira Jain Śaka + 36 years of his rule. If we go by this method, the date of Śaṅkara can be calculated as 3762 + 36 - 2630= 1168 BC, which again supports our hypothesis.

Aparokṣānubhūti

श्रीहरिं परमानन्दमुपदेष्टारमीश्वरम् ।
व्यापकं सर्वलोकानां कारणं तं नमाम्यहम् ॥१ ॥
śrīharim̐ paramānandamupadeṣṭāramīśvaram,
vyāpakam̐ sarvalokānām̐ kāraṇam̐ tam̐ namāmyaham.

1. I bow down to God, the Supreme Bliss, the first Teacher, who hast he potential to create the world, the All-pervading One, and the efficient cause of all Lokas (worlds).

अपरोक्षानुभूतिर्वै प्रोच्यते मोक्षसिद्धये ।
सद्भिरेषा प्रयत्नेन वीक्षणीया मुहुर्मुहुः । ।२ । ।
aparokṣānubhūtirvai prochyate mokṣasiddhaye,
sadbhireṣā prayatnena vīkṣaṇīyā muhurmuhuḥ.

2. In this text, the direct realization of the invisible Brahman for achieving liberation is discussed. Only those with a pure heart should pursue this realization through diligent practice.

स्ववर्णाश्रमधर्मेण तपसा हरितोषणात् ।
साधनं प्रभवेत्पुंसां वैराग्यादिचतुष्टयम् । ।३ । ।
svavarṇāśramadharmeṇa tapasā haritoṣaṇāt,
sādhanam̐ prabhavetpum̐sām̐ vairāgyādichatuṣṭayam.

3. The four preliminary means for realization are: performing duties assigned to one's Varṇa (profession based on Sanskāras) and Āśrama; practicing yoga and austerities; dedicating oneself to God; and detachment to the worldly things (Vairāgya).

ब्रह्मादिस्थावरान्तेषु वैराग्यं विषयेष्वनु ।
यथैव काकविष्ठायां वैराग्यं तद्धि निर्मलम् । ।४ । ।
brahmādisthāvarānteṣu vairāgyam̐ viṣayeṣvanu,

yathaiva kākaviṣṭhāyāṁ vairāgyaṁ taddhi nirmalam.

4. Just as we are detached from a crow's excreta, true detachment from all sensory objects, from the Brahmā to material things, is called pure Vairāgya.

Note: Here Śaṅkara tells that a seeker of mokṣa should detach from any legendry figures called Bhagwan like Brahmā, Śiva, Viṣṇu, Rāma, Kṛṣṇa and others or say desist from their worship.

नित्यमात्मस्वरूपं हि दृश्यं तद्विपरीतगम्।
एवं यो निश्चयः सम्यग्विवेको वस्तुनः स वै।।५।।
nityamātmasvarūpaṁ hi dṛśyaṁ tadviparītagam,
ēvaṁ yo niśchayaḥ samyagviveko vastunaḥ sa vai.

5. By nature, the ātman (soul) is eternal, while the visible body (form) is non-eternal. Those who can discern this can understand the difference between these two.

सदैव वासनात्यागः शमोऽयमिति शब्दितः।
निग्रहो बाह्यवृत्तीनां दम इत्यभिधीयते॥६॥
sadaiva vāsanātyāgaḥ śamo'yamiti śabditaḥ,
nigraho bāhyavṛttīnāṁ dama ityabhidhīyate.

6. Abandoning desires at all times is known as Śama, while withdrawing the mind from external stimuli is called Dama.

विषयेभ्यः परावृत्तिः परमोपरतिर्हि सा।
सहनं सर्वदुःखानां तितिक्षा सा शुभा मता।।७।।
viṣayebhyaḥ parāvṛttiḥ paramoparatirhi sā,
sahanaṁ sarvaduḥkhānāṁ titikṣā sā śubhā matā.

7. Completely turning away from sensory objects is the highest form of Uparati (renunciation), while enduring all sufferings is known as Titikṣā (forbearance), which is deemed beneficial.

निगमाचार्यवाक्येषु भक्तिः श्रद्धेति विश्रुता।
चित्तैकाग्र्यं तु सल्लक्ष्ये समाधानमिति स्मृतम् ॥८॥
nigamāchāryavākyeṣu bhaktiḥ śraddheti viśrutā,
chittaikāgryaṁ tu sallakṣaye samādhānamiti smṛtam.

8. Faith in the words of the Vedas and the Ācharya who teaches Veda is called Śraddhā, while focusing the mind on the ultimate goal (Brahman) is termed Samādhāna.

संसारबन्धनिर्मुक्तिः कथं स्यान्मे दयानिधे।
इति या सुदृढा बुद्धिर्वक्तव्या सा मुमुक्षुता।।९।।
saṁsārabandhanirmuktiḥ kathaṁ syānme dayānidhe,
iti yā sudṛḍhā buddhirvaktavyā sā mumukṣutā.

9. How can I be liberated from the bondage of the world, O compassionate Lord? Such a burning desire is known as Mumukṣutā (qualification for the desire of liberation).

उक्तसाधनयुक्तेन विचारः पुरुषेण हि।
कर्तव्यो ज्ञानसिद्ध्यर्थमात्मनः शुभमिच्छता ॥१०॥
uktasādhanayuktena vichāraḥ puruṣeṇa hi,
kartavyo jñānasiddhyarthamātmanaḥ
śubhamichchhatā.

10. Equipped with the above qualifications for self-realization, a seeker desiring their good (mokṣa) should make quest for understanding the true reality.

नोत्पद्यते विना ज्ञानं विचारेणान्यसाधनैः।
यथा पदार्थभानं हि प्रकाशेन विना क्वचित्।।११।।
notpadyate vinā jñānaṁ vichāreṇānyasādhanaiḥ,
yathā padārthabhānaṁ hi prakāśena vinā kvachit.

11. No self-realization can occur without quest for understanding the true reality, just as the presence of an object cannot be known without the aid of light.

कोऽहं कथमिदं जातं को वा कर्तास्य विद्यते।
उपादानं किमस्तीह विचारः सोऽयमीदृशः ॥१२॥
ko'haṁ kathamidaṁ jātaṁ ko vā kartāsya vidyate,
upādānaṁ kimastīha vichāraḥ so'yamīdṛśaḥ.

12. Who am I? How did this world come into existence? Who is the creator behind it all? What is the material cause of this universe? These profound questions lie at the heart of our quest for understanding.

नाहं भूतगणो देहो नाहं चाक्षगणस्तथा।
एतद्विलक्षणः कश्चिद्विचारः सोऽयमीदृशः ॥१३॥
nāhaṁ bhūtagaṇo deho nāhaṁ chākṣagaṇastathā,
ētadvilakṣaṇaḥ kaśchidvichāraḥ so'yamīdṛśaḥ.

13. I am not simply the body composed of five elements, nor am I just a collection of sensory organs; I am something far greater than these. This realization marks the beginning of true inquiry.

अज्ञानप्रभवं सर्वं ज्ञानेन प्रविलीयते।
संकल्पो विविधः कर्ता विचारः सोऽयमीदृशः ॥१४॥
ajñānaprabhavaṁ sarvaṁ jñānena pravilīyate,
saṁkalpo vividhaḥ kartā vichāraḥ so'yamīdṛśaḥ.

14. Avidyā which refers to the sanskāras of the material world, is the cause of birth. When one identifies the true nature of one's self, all these illusions dissolve. The various types of [saṅkalpa] sanskāras of the material world (desires for material objects) cause the creation of various bodies of different species. This realization marks the quest for understanding the true reality.

एतयोर्यदुपादानमेकं सूक्ष्मं सदव्ययम्।
यथैव मृद्घटादीनां विचारः सोऽयमीदृशः ॥१५॥
ētayoryadupādānamekaṁ sūkṣamaṁ sadavyayam,

yathaiva mṛddhaṭādīnāṁ vichāraḥ so'yamīdṛśaḥ.

15. Avidyā (the knoweldge of the material world) and Saṅkalpa (the desire for material objects) are based upon a single subtle and eternal prakṛti, the material cause oft he universe, similar to how clay serves as the material cause for a pot and other objects. This illustrates the direction of the quest.

अहमेकोऽपि सूक्ष्मश्च ज्ञाता साक्षी सदव्ययः ।
तदहं नात्र संदेहो विचारः सोऽयमीदृशः ॥१६ ॥
ahameko'pi sūkṣamaścha jñātā sākṣī sadavyayaḥ,
tadahaṁ nātra saṁdeho vichāraḥ so'yamīdṛśaḥ.

16. I am a singular entity: the subtle, the knower, the witness, the ever-existent, and the unchanging. There is no doubt that my true nature is as such. This is what is the direction of the quest.

आत्मा विनिष्कलो ह्येको देहो बहुभिरावृतः ।
तयोरैक्यं प्रपश्यन्ति किमज्ञानमतः परम् ॥१७ ॥
ātmā viniṣkalo hyeko deho bahubhirāvṛtaḥ,
tayoraikyaṁ prapaśyanti kimajñānamataḥ param.

17. Ātman is fundamentally one and without division, while the body is composed of many distinct parts; yet many people mistakenly perceive these two as a singular entity. What could be a more profound ignorance than this?

आत्मा नियामकश्चान्तर्देहो नियम्यबाह्यकः ।
तयोरैक्यं प्रपश्यन्ति किमज्ञानमतः परम् ॥१८ ॥
ātmā niyāmakaśchāntardeho niyamyabāhyakaḥ,
tayoraikyaṁ prapaśyanti kimajñānamataḥ param.

18. Ātman is the ruler of the body and is internal, the body is the ruled and is external; yet many people

mistakenly perceive these two as a singular entity. What could be a more profound ignorance than this?

आत्मा ज्ञानमयः पुण्यो देहो मांसमयोऽशुचिः ।
तयोरैक्यं प्रपश्यन्ति किमज्ञानमतः परम् ॥१९॥
ātmā jñānamayaḥ puṇyo deho māṁsamayo'śuchiḥ,
tayoraikyaṁ prapaśyanti kimajñānamataḥ param.

19. Ātman is chetana (immaterial) and holy, the body is all made of flesh and impure; yet many people mistakenly perceive these two as a singular entity. What could be a more profound ignorance than this?

आत्मा प्रकाशकः स्वच्छो देहस्तामस उच्यते ।
तयोरैक्यं प्रपश्यन्ति किमज्ञानमतः परम् ॥२०॥
ātmā prakāśakaḥ svachchho dehastāmasa uchyate,
tayoraikyaṁ prapaśyanti kimajñānamataḥ param.

20. Ātman is the illuminator and pure sāttvika, whereas the body is of the nature of tamas. However, people mistakenly perceive these two as a singular entity. What could be a deeper ignorance than this?

आत्मा नित्यो हि सद्रूपो देहोऽनित्यो ह्यसन्मयः ।
तयोरैक्यं प्रपश्यन्ति किमज्ञानमतः परम् ॥२१॥
ātmā nityo hi sadrūpo deho'nityo hyasanmayaḥ,
tayoraikyaṁ prapaśyanti kimajñānamataḥ param.

21. Ātman is eternal, ever-existent; the body is non-eternal and perishable. However, people are not able to discriminate between the two. What could be a deeper ignorance than this?

आत्मनस्तत्प्रकाशत्वं यत्पदार्थावभासनम् ।
नाग्न्यादिदीप्तिवद्दीप्तिर्भवत्यान्ध्यं यतो निशि ।।२२।।
ātmanastatprakāśatvaṁ yatpadārthāvabhāsanam,
nāgnyādidīptivaddīptirbhavatyāndhyaṁ yato niśi.

22. The illuminatorship of the self, or Ātman, is clearly evident in our ability to perceive objects around us. This light transcends the mere glow of fire or any other source; even when lights are present, darkness can still envelop certain placcs at night. This distinction underscores the profound nature of Ātman's illuminative power, highlighting that true illumination comes from within.

Note: A dead body is not able to perceive anything.

देहोऽहमित्ययं मूढो मत्वा तिष्ठत्यहो जनः ।
ममायमित्यपि ज्ञात्वा घटद्रष्टेव सर्वदा ॥२३ ॥
deho'hamityayaṁ mūḍho matvā tiṣṭhatyaho janaḥ,
mamāyamityapi jñātvā ghaṭadraṣṭeva sarvadā.

23. A fool is content with believing he is the body, while he knows, as the owner, that this body belongs to him.

ब्रह्मैवाहं समः शान्तः सच्चिदानन्दलक्षणः ।
नाहं देहो ह्यसद्रूपो ज्ञानमित्युच्यते बुधैः ॥२४ ॥
brahmaivāhaṁ samaḥ śāntaḥ sachchidānandalakṣaṇaḥ,
nāhaṁ deho hyasadrūpo jñānamityuchyate budhaiḥ.

24. I am verily the soul, being [samaḥ] equanimous, [śāntaḥ] quiescent, and by nature [sat] eternal, [chit] chetana, and [ānandaḥ] blissful. I am not the body which is [asat+rūpaḥ] perishable. This is called true knowledge by the wise.

निर्विकारो निराकारो निरवद्योऽहमव्ययः ।
नाहं देहो ह्यसद्रूपो ज्ञानमित्युच्यते बुधैः ।।२५।।
nirvikāro nirākāro niravadyo'hamavyayaḥ,
nāhaṁ deho hyasadrūpo jñānamityuchyate budhaiḥ.

25. I am without any change, without any form, free from all blemish and [avyaḥ] decay. I am not the body

which is perishable. This is called true knowledge by the wise.

निरामयो निराभासो निर्विकल्पोऽहमाततः ।
नाहं देहो ह्यसद्रूपो ज्ञानमित्युच्यते बुधैः ॥२६ ॥
nirāmayo nirābhāso nirvikalpo'hamātataḥ,
nāhaṁ deho hyasadrūpo jñānamityuchyate budhaiḥ.

26. I am not subject to any disease, I am invisible, [nirvikalpaḥ] free from all changes and [atataḥ] pervade any type of body (human, animal or other). I am not the body which is perishablen. This is called true knowledge by the wise.

निर्गुणो निष्क्रियो नित्यो नित्यमुक्तोऽहमच्युतः ।
नाहं देहो ह्यसद्रूपो ज्ञानमित्युच्यते बुधैः ॥२७ ॥
nirguṇo niṣkriyo nityo nityamukto'hamachyutaḥ,
nāhaṁ deho hyasadrūpo jñānamityuchyate budhaiḥ.

27. I am [nirguṇaḥ] devoid of attributes which can be assigned to material objects, I am [niṣkriyaḥ] motionless, eternal and [achyutaḥ] imperishable. I am not the body which is perishable. This is called true knowledge by the wise.

निर्मलो निश्चलोऽनन्तः शुद्धोऽहमजरोऽमरः ।
नाहं देहो ह्यसद्रूपो ज्ञानमित्युच्यते बुधैः ।।२८।।
nirmalo niśchalo'nantaḥ śuddho'hamajaro'maraḥ,
nāhaṁ deho hyasadrūpo jñānamityuchyate budhaiḥ.

28. I am free from all impurity, I am motionless, endless, holy, undecaying, and immortal. I am not the body which is perishable. This is called true knowledge by the wise.

स्वदेहं शोभनं त्यक्त्वा पुरुषाख्यं च संमतम् ।
किं मूर्ख शून्यमात्मानं देहातीतं करोषि भो ॥२९ ॥

svadehaṁ śobhanaṁ tyaktvā puruṣākhyaṁ cha saṁmatam,
kiṁ mūrkha śūnyamātmānaṁ dehātītaṁ karoṣi bho.

29. [Mūrkha] O, misguided one! [tyaktvā] When you abandon the [śobhanam] radiant ātman, [dehāttam] the essence that transcends the physical form and [puruṣākhyam] is referred to as puruṣa in the Śāstras, [svadehaṁ kiṁ karoṣi bho!] what fate awaits a body [śunyam ātmānam] stripped of its soul?

स्वात्मानं श्रृणु मूर्ख त्वं श्रुत्या युक्त्या च पूरुषम् ।
देहातीतं सदाकारं सुदुर्दर्शं भवादृशाम् ॥३० ॥
svātmānaṁ śrṛṇu mūrkha tvaṁ śrutyā yuktyā cha pūruṣam,
dehātītaṁ sadākāraṁ sudurdarśaṁ bhavādṛśām.

30. O, ignorant one! Try to know, with the help of Śruti and reasoning, your own self, called Puruṣa, which is beyond the body, eternal by nature, and very difficult for persons like you to realize.

अहंशब्देन विख्यात एक एव स्थितः परः ।
स्थूलत्वान्नैकतां प्राप्तः कथं स्याद्देहकः पुमान् ॥३१ ॥
ahaṁśabdena vikhyāta ēka ēva sthitaḥ paraḥ,
sthūlatvānnaikatāṁ prāptaḥ kathaṁ syāddehakaḥ pumān.

31. [dehakaḥ pumān] The Soul, [vikhyātaḥ] referred to [ahaṁśabdena] by the term "Aham," [paraḥ sthitaḥ] transcends the body and exists [eka eva] as a singular entity in the body, while [dehakaḥ] the body [sthūlatvāt] being inherently material [na+ekatāṁ prāptaḥ] is not one, but made of many components. So, [katham] how can this body [syāt] be the soul?

अहं द्रष्टृतया सिद्धो देहो दृश्यतया स्थितः ।

ममायमिति निर्देशात्कथं स्याद्देहकः पुमान् ॥३२ ॥
ahaṁ draṣṭṛtayā siddho deho dṛśyatayā sthitaḥ,
mamāyamiti nirdeśātkathaṁ syāddehakaḥ pumān.

32. "Aham" (soul) is well established as the seer (witness) whereas the body is the sight. This is learnt from the fact that when we address the body we say, "This is mine." So how can this body be Puruṣa?

अहं विकारहीनस्तु देहो नित्यं विकारवान् ।
इति प्रतीयते साक्षात्कथं स्याद्देहकः पुमान् । ।३३ । ।
ahaṁ vikārahīnastu deho nityaṁ vikāravān,
iti pratīyate sākṣātkathaṁ syāddehakaḥ pumān.

33. It is a fact of direct experience that the "Aham" remains unchanging and eternal, while the body is in a state of constant flux. Given this fundamental difference, how can we regard this impermanent body as Puruṣa?

यस्मात्परमिति श्रुत्या तया पुरुषलक्षणम् ।
विनिर्णीतं विशुद्धेन कथं स्याद्देहकः पुमान् । ।३४ । ।
yasmātparamiti śrutyā tayā puruṣalakṣaṇam,
vinirṇītaṁ viśuddhena kathaṁ syāddehakaḥ pumān.

34. Esteemed scholars have revealed the profound essence of Puruṣa through the Śruti text that states, "There is nothing higher than Puruṣa in the body." Given this insight, how can we reconcile the idea that this body is, in fact, Puruṣa?

सर्वं पुरुष एवेति सूक्ते पुरुषसंज्ञिते ।
अप्युच्यते यतः श्रुत्या कथं स्याद्देहकः पुमान् ॥३५ ॥
sarvaṁ puruṣa ēveti sūkte puruṣasaṁjñite,
apyuchyate yataḥ śrutyā kathaṁ syāddehakaḥ pumān.

35. The Śruti emphatically asserts in the Puruṣa Sūkta that "All physical bodies are pervaded by the Puruṣa."

Given this profound declaration, how can we possibly claim that this physical body is the Puruṣa?

असङ्गः पुरुषः प्रोक्तो बृहदारण्यकेऽपि च।
अनन्तमलसंसृष्टः कथं स्याद्देहकः पुमान् ॥३६॥
asaṅgaḥ puruṣaḥ prokto bṛhadāraṇyake'pi cha,
anantamalasaṁsṛṣṭaḥ kathaṁ syāddehakaḥ pumān.

36. In the Bṛhadāraṇyaka Upaniṣad, it is declared that "The Puruṣa is entirely pure and unattached." This raises a question: how can a body so laden with countless impurities be identified as the Puruṣa?

तत्रैव च समाख्यातः स्वयंज्योतिर्हि पूरुषः।
जडः परप्रकाश्योऽयं कथं स्याद्देहकः पुमान् ॥३७॥
tatraiva cha samākhyātaḥ svayaṁjyotirhi pūruṣaḥ,
jaḍaḥ paraprakāśyo'yaṁ kathaṁ syāddehakaḥ pumān.

37. It is unequivocally stated that "the Puruṣa is self-illumined." Given this, how can the inert (material) body—merely illuminated by an external agent—truly be considered the Puruṣa?

प्रोक्तोऽपि कर्मकाण्डेन ह्यात्मा देहाद्विलक्षणः।
नित्यश्च तत्फलं भुङ्क्ते देहपातादनन्तरम्।।३८।।
prokto'pi karmakāṇḍena hyātmā dehādvilakṣaṇaḥ,
nityaścha tatphalaṁ bhuṅkte dehapātādanantaram.

38. Furthermore, the principle of Karma asserts that the Ātman, or the true self, is fundamentally different from the physical body and is everlasting, as it continues to exist even after the body dies and experiences the consequences of actions performed in this life.

लिङ्गं चानेकसंयुक्तं चलं दृश्यं विकारि च।
अव्यापकमसद्रूपं तत्कथं स्यात्पुमानयम् ॥३९॥
liṅgaṁ chānekasaṁyuktaṁ chalaṁ dṛśyaṁ vikāri cha,

avyāpakamasadrūpaṁ tatkathaṁ syātpumānayam.

39. The physical body, composed of numerous parts, is inherently movable. As an object of perception, it is subject to change, limited in nature, and ultimately non-eternal. Given these characteristics, how can one truly regard this as the Puruṣa?

एवं देहद्वयादन्य आत्मा पुरुष ईश्वरः ।
सर्वात्मा सर्वरूपश्च सर्वातीतोऽहमव्ययः ॥४० ॥
ēvaṁ dehadvayādanya ātmā puruṣa īśvaraḥ,
sarvātmā sarvarūpaścha sarvātīto'hamavyayaḥ.

40. [Evam] Thus [ātmā] Brahman or [puruṣaḥ] Puruṣa (Viśeṣa) [anyaḥ] different [dehadvayāt] from both the soul and body is called [Iśvaraḥ] Īśvara or God. He pervades [sarvātma] all souls and [sarvarūpaḥ] all forms, [sarvātītaḥ] yet transends them all, He is also named as "Aham" and [avyayaḥ] unchangeable.

Note: In this profound discussion, Śri Śaṅkarāchārya clarifies the distinction between puruṣa or ātmā as understood within the duality principle of Sāṅkhya and the elevated concept of Puruṣa or Ātmā identified as Īśvara. He powerfully underscores that these terms, Ātmā and Puruṣa, carry dual significance: one pertains to the individual soul, while the other embodies the divine essence of God. This insight invites a deeper understanding of the interconnectedness of the self and the ultimate reality. He also clarifies here that the word 'Aham' is used only for Brahman (God) or sometime for soul, not for any human being or human body.

इत्यात्मदेहभानेन प्रपञ्चस्यैव सत्यता ।
यथोक्ता तर्कशास्त्रेण ततः किं पुरुषार्थता ॥४१ ॥
ityātmadehabhānena prapañchasyaiva satyatā,

yathoktā tarkaśāstreṇa tataḥ kiṁ puruṣārthatā.

41. [ātma-deha-bhānena] The body is expressed through Ātman, [prapañchasya+eva satyatā] reflecting the reality of the phenomenal world, [yathoktā] as outlined in the [tarkaśāstreṇa] Tarkaśāstra (Śāṅkhya Śāstra, etc.]. Apart from this understanding, what else defines the purpose of human life?

इत्यात्मदेहभेदेन देहात्मत्वं निवारितम्।
इदानीं देहभेदस्य ह्यसत्त्वं स्फुटमुच्यते ॥४२ ॥
ityātmadehabhedena dehātmatvaṁ nivāritam,
idānīṁ dehabhedasya hyasattvaṁ sphuṭamuchyate.

42. Thus, the distinction between ātman (soul) and deha (body) indicates that the body is not the Atman. The the separation between the unreal body and ātman is now clearly explained.

Thus, the distinction between ātman (soul) and deha (body) underscores the assertion that the body is not the Ātman.

चैतन्यस्यैकरूपत्वाद्भेदो युक्तो न कर्हिचित्।
जीवत्वं च मृषा ज्ञेयं रज्ज्वां सर्पग्रहो यथा ॥४३ ॥
chaitanyasyaikarūpatvādbhedo yukto na karhichit,
jīvatvaṁ cha mṛṣā jñeyaṁ rajjvāṁ sarpagraho yathā.

43. [na bhedaḥ] No division [chaitanyasya] of Chaitanya element (Brahman) [yuktaḥ] is admissible [karhichit] at any time [ekarūpatvāt] as it is always one and the same. [cha] So, [jīvatvam] its (Brahman's) transformation into jīva (embodied soul) must be known as false, like the delusion of a snake in a rope.

Note: Śaṅkara asserts that Brahman is consistently unchanging at all times, making the idea of His many division and transformation into embodied souls (jīvas) is a misconception.

Thus we can say that the great Śaṅkara powerfully asserts that Brahman is eternally unchanging, emphasizing that the belief in His transformation into embodied souls (jīvas) is fundamentally misguided. This profound understanding reveals the nature of reality, urging us to grasp the truth of Brahman's unyielding unity.

रज्ज्वज्ञानात्क्षणेनैव यद्वद्रज्जुर्हि सर्पिणी।
भाति तद्वच्चितिः साक्षाद्विश्वाकारेण केवला ॥४४॥
rajjvajñānātkṣaṇenaiva yadvadrajjurhi sarpiṇī,
bhāti tadvachchitiḥ sākṣādviśvākāreṇa kevalā.

44. [yat+vat] As [rajju+ajñānāt] due to the lack of understanding the real material nature of the rope, [rajjuḥ+hi] the very rope [bhāti] appears [kṣaṇena+eva] instantly as [sarpiṇī] an immaterial snake, [tat+vat] so also does [chitiḥ] pure immaterial Brahman appears [sākṣāt] directly [viśvākāreṇa] transforming in the visible material world by an ignorant (Neo-Vedāntins).

Note: In this statement, the esteemed Śaṅkara underscores a crucial distinction: it is not Brahman that manifests as the material visible world during creation. Rather, it is prakṛti that undergoes this transformative process into the tangible universe we perceive. Consequently, the Neo-Vedāntins promote a misguided interpretation while unjustly invoking the authority of Ādi Śaṅkara Āchārya. This misrepresentation must be challenged, as it diverges from the foundational truths of Vedantic philosophy.

उपादानं प्रपञ्चस्य ब्रह्मणोऽन्यन्न विद्यते।
तस्मात्सर्वप्रपञ्चोऽयं ब्रह्मैवास्ति न चेतरत् ॥४५॥
upādānaṁ prapañchasya brahmaṇo'nyanna vidyate,

tasmātsarvaprapañcho'yaṁ brahmaivāsti na chetarat.

45. No other efficient [upādāna] cause of this phenomenal universe exists besides Brahman. Thus, this entire universe is created by Brahman and nothing else.

व्याप्यव्यापकता मिथ्या सर्वमात्मेति शासनात् ।
इति ज्ञाते परे तत्त्वे भेदस्यावसरः कुतः ॥४६ ॥
vyāpyavyāpakatā mithyā sarvamātmeti śāsanāt,
iti jñāte pare tattve bhedasyāvasaraḥ kutaḥ.

46. According to declarations from Śruti texts, such as "Every living being is not the body but the soul," when the Supreme Truth (Brahman) is realized and mokṣa is attained, the concept of the soul being pervaded by Brahman becomes irrelevant. In mokṣa, there is no visible distinction between Brahman and the liberated soul.

श्रुत्या निवारितं नूनं नानात्वं स्वमुखेन हि ।
कथं भासो भवेदन्यः स्थिते चाद्वयकारणे ॥४७ ॥
śrutyā nivāritaṁ nūnaṁ nānātvaṁ svamukhena hi,
kathaṁ bhāso bhavedanyaḥ sthite chādvayakāraṇe.

47. Indeed, the Śruti texts have directly [nivāritam] denied [nānātvam] manifoldness in Brahman (Brahman is always the same). [katham] How can he [anyaḥ bhāsaḥ] appear differently from his actual nature by manifesting into the visible universe, when prakṛti as the [advayakāriṇe] sole material cause of creation [sthite] exists?

Note: Here Śri Śaṅkara Āchārya asserts that Brahman is unchangeable in all times, so He needs not manifest in a multiform universe when prakṛti is there as the material cause of the universe.

दोषोऽपि विहितः श्रुत्या मृत्योर्मृत्युं स गच्छति ।

इह पश्यति नानात्वं मायया वञ्चितो नरः ॥४८ ॥
doṣo'pi vihitaḥ śrutyā mṛtyormṛtyuṁ sa gachchhati,
iha paśyati nānātvaṁ māyayā vañchito naraḥ.

48. The Śruti texts say that a jīva (embodied soul) trapped in evil attains death after death and undergoes experiencing bodies of various species being deceived by the attractions of [māyayā] material world.

ब्रह्मणः सर्वभूतानि जायन्ते परमात्मनः ।
तस्मादेतानि ब्रह्मैव भवन्तीत्यवधारयेत् ॥४९ ॥
brahmaṇaḥ sarvabhūtāni jāyante paramātmanaḥ,
tasmādetāni brahmaiva bhavantītyavadhārayet.

49. Inasmuch as all beings (souls) are born of Brahman, the Paramātman, their ultimate goal of life is to attain Brahman (mokṣa).

ब्रह्मैव सर्वनामानि रूपाणि विविधानि च ।
कर्माण्यपि समग्राणि बिभर्तीति श्रुतिर्जगौ ॥५० ॥
brahmaiva sarvanāmāni rūpāṇi vividhāni cha,
karmāṇyapi samagrāṇi bibhartīti śrutirjagau.

50. The Śruti texts says that that [sarva-nāmāni, vividhāni, rūpāṇi karmāvi cha] all varieties of names, forms, and actions are given [brahmaiva] based upon Vedas.

सुवर्णाज्जायमानस्य सुवर्णत्वं च शाश्वतम् ।
ब्रह्मणो जायमानस्य ब्रह्मत्वं च तथा भवेत् ॥५१ ॥
suvarṇājjāyamānasya suvarṇatvaṁ cha śāśvatam,
brahmaṇo jāyamānasya brahmatvaṁ cha tathā bhavet.

51. Just as a product of gold inherently embodies the qualities of gold, a soul that emerges from Brahman is destined to reflect the essence of Brahman itself. This profound connection emphasizes that the true nature of

the soul is aligned with achieving mokṣa, or liberation.

स्वल्पमप्यन्तरं कृत्वा जीवात्मपरमात्मनोः ।
योऽवतिष्ठति मूढात्मा भयं तस्याभिभाषितम् ।।५२।।
svalpamapyantaraṁ kṛtvā jīvātmaparamātmanoḥ,
yo'vatiṣṭhati mūḍhātmā bhayaṁ tasyābhibhāṣitam.

52. As long as an ignorant one remains distant from Brahman (not having attained mokṣa), the texts clearly indicate they will be plagued by fears of both pain and pleasure.

यत्राज्ञानाद्भवेद्द्वैतमितरस्तत्र पश्यति ।
आत्मत्वेन यदा सर्वं नेतरस्तत्र चाण्वपि ।।५३।।
yatrājñānādbhaveddvaitamitarastatra paśyati,
ātmatvena yadā sarvaṁ netarastatra chāṇvapi.

53. [yatra] When [ajñānāt] due to ignorance, souls are viewed as [dvaitam] endowed with different natures, then the distinction between souls [bhavet] appears, and one soul [paśyati] finds itself [itaraḥ] different from others; but when [sarvam] all souls are viewed [ātmatvena] having the same nature (soul), no difference [aṇvapi] even the slightest one is experienced (all souls being of the same nature).

यस्मिन्सर्वाणि भूतानि ह्यात्मत्वेन विजानतः ।
न वै तस्य भवेन्मोहो न च शोकोऽद्वितीयतः ।।५४।।
yasminsarvāṇi bhūtāni hyātmatvena vijānataḥ,
na vai tasya bhavenmoho na cha śoko'dvitīyataḥ.

54. [yasmin] In the state when one [vijānataḥ] identifies [sarvāṇi bhūtāni] all living beings [ātmatvena] with their essence Ātman (soul), there arises neither [mohaḥ] delusion nor sorrow, [adviyataḥ] from the other soul (jīvas) which has the same nature.

अयमात्मा हि ब्रह्मैव सर्वात्मकतया स्थितः ।
इति निर्धारितं श्रुत्या बृहदारण्यसंस्थया ।।५५।।
ayamātmā hi brahmaiva sarvātmakatayā sthitaḥ,
iti nirdhāritaṁ śrutyā bṛhadāraṇyasaṁsthayā.

55. The Bṛhadāraṇyaka Upaniṣad has declared that this ātman (spiritual element), which is [sarvātmatayā sthitaḥ] located in all bodies, [brahmaiva] is verily called Brahman.

Note: When Ātman (individual being) is referred to as Brahman, then Supreme being is known by the designation of Parabrahman. It is important to understand the distinction between Ātman (the soul) and Brahman (God). In our texts, soul and God are equally referred to as Brahman. This overlap can lead to confusion. Therefore, it is essential to interpret the term Brahman as Ātman and Brahman according to the context in which they are used.

अनुभूतोऽप्ययं लोको व्यवहारक्षमोऽपि सन् ।
असद्रूपो यथा स्वप्न उत्तरक्षणबाधतः ॥५६॥
anubhūto'pyayaṁ loko vyavahārakṣamo'pi san,
asadrūpo yathā svapna uttarakṣaṇabādhataḥ.

56. This world, though an object of our daily experience and serving all practical purposes for attaining mokṣa, is, like the dream world, of the perishable nature, inasmuch as it is changing every next moment.

स्वप्नो जागरणेऽलीकः स्वप्नेऽपि न हि जागरः ।
द्वयमेव लये नास्ति लयोऽपि ह्युभयोर्न च ।।५७।।
svapno jāgaraṇe'līkaḥ svapne'pi na hi jāgaraḥ,
dvayameva laye nāsti layo'pi hyubhayorna cha.

57. The experience of a dream is unreal (not experienced) in waking, whereas the experience of waking is absent in a dream. Both, however, are non-

existent in deep sleep, which, again, is not experienced in either.

Note: Here, Śri Śaṅkara has equated the dream state with the creation, an awaking state with the state of self-realization, and laya (deep sleep) with mokṣa. So the experience of the phenomenal world is not experienced in the state of self-realization and the experience of self-realization is absent in the phenomenal world. Both experiences are absent in the state of mokṣa.

त्रयमेवं भवेन्मिथ्या गुणत्रयविनिर्मितम्।
अस्य द्रष्टा गुणातीतो नित्यो ह्येकश्चिदात्मकः।।५८।।
trayamevaṁ bhavenmithyā guṇatrayavinirmitam,
asya draṣṭā guṇātīto nityo hyekaśchidātmakaḥ.

58. The three states of body-waking, dreaming and deep sleep are unreal as they are the creation of the three Guṇas; however, their witness (soul) is eternal, one, beyond all Guṇas, and immaterial.

यद्वन्मृदि घटभ्रान्तिं शुक्तौ वा रजतस्थितिम्।
तद्वद्ब्रह्मणि जीवत्वं भ्रान्त्या पश्यति न स्वतः।।५९।।
yadvanmṛdi ghaṭabhrāntiṁ śuktau vā rajatasthitim,
tadvadbrahmaṇi jīvatvaṁ bhrāntyā paśyati na svataḥ.

59. [yadvat] Just as the [mṛdi ghaṭ bhrāntiṁ] deluded one sees a pot in earth or [rajat sthitim] silver in [śuktau] the oyster shell, so does one considers [brahmaṇi] Brahman as [jīvatvam] Jīva [bhrāntyā] due to delusion, [na svataḥ] but not when the Brahman is realized.

Note: The author asserts that despite the fact that pot is composed of earth, they possess distinct forms and characteristics. Similarly, although souls originate from Brahman, they are fundamentally different from one another. The soul and Brahman are not one and the same entities.

यथा मृदि घटो नाम कनके कुण्डलाभिधा।
शुक्तौ हि रजतख्यातिर्जीवशब्दस्तथा परे।।६०।।
yathā mṛdi ghaṭo nāma kanake kuṇḍalābhidhā,
śuktau hi rajatakhyātirjīvaśabdastathā pare.

60. Just as a pot exists in earth, ear-ring in gold, and silver in oyster shell, so does the soul in Brahman.

यथैव व्योम्नि नीलत्वं यथा नीरं मरुस्थले।
पुरुषत्वं यथा स्थाणौ तद्वद्विश्वं चिदात्मनि।।६१।।
yathaiva vyomni nīlatvaṁ yathā nīraṁ marusthale,
puruṣatvaṁ yathā sthāṇau tadvadviśvaṁ chidātmani.

61. Just as blueness is reflected in the sky (blueness though exists independently, but does not find its origin in the sky), water in the mirage (water has its independent existence, but does not have its origin in the mirage), and a human figure in a post (human figure exists independently, but does find its origin in the post), so does the universe in Brahman. The universe exists independently but does not find its origin in Brahman.

यथैव शून्ये वेतालो गन्धर्वाणां पुरं यथा।
यथाकाशे द्विचन्द्रत्वं तद्वत्सत्ये जगत्स्थितिः ॥६२॥
yathaiva śūnye vetālo gandharvāṇāṁ puraṁ yathā,
yathākāśe dvichandratvaṁ tadvatsatye jagatsthitiḥ.

62. Just as the appearance of a ghost in an empty place, of a castle in the air, and a second moon in the sky (is an illusion, not the reality), so is the appearance of the universe in Brahman is an illusion of Neo-Vedantins, not the reality. The universe originates from Prakṛti.

यथा तरङ्गकल्लोलैर्जलमेव स्फुरत्यलम्।
पात्ररूपेण ताम्रं हि ब्रह्माण्डौघैस्तथात्मता ॥६३॥

yathā taraṅgakallolairjalameva sphuratyalaṁ,
pātrarūpeṇa tāmraṁ hi brahmāṇḍaughaistathātmatā.

63. Just as through ripples and waves, the presence of water is known, through the vessel of copper, the presence of copper can be experienced, similarly from the multitude of Brahmaṇḍas (universes), the presence of Brahman, as the creator, can be known.

घटनाम्ना यथा पृथ्वी पटनाम्ना हि तन्तवः ।
जगन्नाम्ना चिदाभाति ज्ञेयं तत्तदभावतः ।।६४।।
ghaṭanāmnā yathā pṛthvī paṭanāmnā hi tantavaḥ,
jagannāmnā chidābhāti jñeyaṁ tattadabhāvataḥ.

64. Just as the existence of earth is known by the pot, the existence of threads by a cloth, so the existence of Brahman is known by the universe. However, the true nature of Brahman exists beyond this material world.

Note: This material world serves to enhance our understanding of Brahman, but it is not the manifestation of Brahman as is viewed by Neo-Vedāntins. Brahman exists beyond this material realm.

सर्वोऽपि व्यवहारस्तु ब्रह्मणा क्रियते जनैः ।
अज्ञानान्न विजानन्ति मृदेव हि घटादिकम् ।।६५।।
sarvo'pi vyavahārastu brahmaṇā kriyate janaiḥ,
ajñānānna vijānanti mṛdeva hi ghaṭādikam.

65. All actions are performed by the body through the inspiration of the soul. However, due to ignorance, we are not aware of this, just as people are unaware of the fact that pots are made by potters with the help of earth.

कार्यकारणता नित्यमास्ते घटमृदोर्यथा ।
तथैव श्रुतियुक्तिभ्यां प्रपञ्चब्रह्मणोरिह ॥६६॥
kāryakāraṇatā nityamāste ghaṭamṛdoryathā,

tathaiva śrutiyuktibhyāṁ prapañchabrahmaṇoriha.

66. Just as there ever exists the relation of material cause and effect between earth and a pot, so does the relation of efficient cause and effect exist between Brahman and the phenomenal world; this has been established here on the strength of Vedic Texts and reasoning.

गृह्यमाणे घटे यद्वन्मृत्तिका भाति वै बलात्।
वीक्ष्यमाणे प्रपञ्चेऽपि ब्रह्मैवाभाति भासुरम्।।६७।।
gṛhyamāṇe ghaṭe yadvanmṛttikā bhāti vai balāt,
vīkṣayamāṇe prapañche'pi brahmaivābhāti bhāsuram.

67. Just as the existence of the earth comes to our mind forcefully while dealing with an earthen pot, the idea of the ever-shining Brahman also flashes in our minds when we have a glimpse of the phenomenal world.

सदैवात्मा विशुद्धोऽपि ह्यशुद्धो भाति वै सदा।
यथैव द्विविधा रज्जुर्ज्ञानिनोऽज्ञानिनोऽनिशम्।।६८।।
sadaivātmā viśuddho'pi hyaśuddho bhāti vai sadā,
yathaiva dvividhā rajjurjñānino'jñānino'niśam.

68. Ātman, though always pure to a wise person, appears impure to the ignorant, just as a rope is perceived differently by the knowledgeable and the uninformed.

यथैव मृन्मयः कुम्भस्तद्वद्देहोऽपि चिन्मयः।
आत्मानात्मविभागोऽयं मुधैव क्रियते बुधैः।।६९।।
yathaiva mṛnmayaḥ kumbhastadvaddeho'pi chinmayaḥ,
ātmānātmavibhāgo'yaṁ mudhaiva kriyate budhaiḥ.

69. Just as a pot is the product of particles of earth, the body is the product of the karmas of the soul. Therefore, the distinction between the soul and the body, as

perceived by the wise, is unhelpful until the soul takes actions that separate it from the body.

सर्पत्वेन यथा रज्जू रजतत्वेन शुक्तिका।
विनिर्णीता विमूढेन देहत्वेन तथात्मता।।७०।।
sarpatvena yathā rajjū rajatatvena śuktikā,
vinirṇītā vimūḍhena dehatvena tathātmatā.

70. Just as a rope is mistakenly perceived as a snake and an oyster shell as a piece of silver, so is the Ātman mistakenly identified with the body by an ignorant person.

घटत्वेन यथा पृथ्वी पटत्वेनैव तन्तवः।
विनिर्णीता विमूढेन देहत्वेन तथात्मता॥७१॥
ghaṭatvena yathā pṛthvī paṭatvenaiva tantavaḥ,
vinirṇītā vimūḍhena dehatvena tathātmatā.

71. Just as the earth is defined by the existence of a pot, threads are defined by a cloth, and Ātman is defined by the body to the informed.

Note: The term vimūḍha has two meanings: ignorant as well as informed.

कनकं कुण्डलत्वेन तरङ्गत्वेन वै जलम्।
विनिर्णीता विमूढेन देहत्वेन तथात्मता।।७२।।
kanakaṁ kuṇḍalatvena taraṅgatvena vai jalam,
vinirṇītā vimūḍhena dehatvena tathātmatā.

72. Just as gold is identified by an ear-ring and water by the waves, so is the Atman identified by body, by the informed.

पुरुषत्वेन वै स्थाणुर्जलत्वेन मरीचिका।
विनिर्णीता विमूढेन देहत्वेन तथात्मता॥७३॥
puruṣatvena vai sthāṇurjalatvena marīchikā,
vinirṇītā vimūḍhena dehatvena tathātmatā.

73. Just as the post is mistaken for a human figure and a mirage for water, so is the body by Ātman, by the ignorant one.

गृहत्वेनैव काष्ठानि खड्गत्वेनैव लोहता।
विनिर्णीता विमूढेन देहत्वेन तथात्मता।।७४।।
gṛhatvenaiva kāṣṭhāni khaṅgatvenaiva lohatā,
vinirṇītā vimūḍhena dehatvena tathātmatā.

74. The type of wood used in constructing a house reflects the quality of a house. Similarly, the quality of a sword indicates the quality of the iron used in its production. Likewise, the bodies of different species provide insight into the quality of the actions (karmas) performed by the soul.

यथा वृक्षविपर्यासो जलाद्भवति कस्यचित्।
तद्वदात्मनि देहत्वं पश्यत्यज्ञानयोगतः ॥७५॥
yathā vṛkṣaviparyāso jalādbhavati kasyachit,
tadvadātmani dehatvaṁ paśyatyajñānayogataḥ.

75. Just as one sees a tree overturned in the water, so a person, because of ignorance, perceives Ātman in body.

पोतेन गच्छतः पुंसः सर्वं भातीव चञ्चलम्।
तद्वदात्मनि देहत्वं पश्यत्यज्ञानयोगतः ॥७६॥
potena gachchhataḥ puṁsaḥ sarvaṁ bhātīva chañchalam,
tadvadātmani dehatvaṁ paśyatyajñānayogataḥ.

76. Just as to a person going in a ship, everything appears to be in motion, so does one perceive Ātman in body.

पीतत्वं हि यथा शुभ्रे दोषाद्भवति कस्यचित्।
तद्वदात्मनि देहत्वं पश्यत्यज्ञानयोगतः ॥७७॥
pītatvaṁ hi yathā śubhre doṣādbhavati kasyachit,

tadvadātmani dehatvaṁ paśyatyajñānayogataḥ.

77. Just as a person with jaundice sees yellow in white things, so does one mistakenly identify Ātman with the body due to ignorance.

चक्षुर्भ्यां भ्रमशीलाभ्यां सर्वं भाति भ्रमात्मकम्।
तद्वदात्मनि देहत्वं पश्यत्यज्ञानयोगतः ॥७८॥
chakṣurbhyāṁ bhramaśīlābhyāṁ sarvaṁ bhāti bhramātmakam,
tadvadātmani dehatvaṁ paśyatyajñānayogataḥ.

78. Just as a person with defective eyes sees things wandering unsteadily, so does one mistakenly identify Ātman with the body due to ignorance.

अलातं भ्रमणेनैव वर्तुलं भाति सूर्यवत्।
तद्वदात्मनि देहत्वं पश्यत्यज्ञानयोगतः ॥७९॥
alātaṁ bhramaṇenaiva vartulaṁ bhāti sūryavat,
tadvadātmani dehatvaṁ paśyatyajñānayogataḥ.

79. Just as a firebrand, through mere rotation, appears circular like the sun, so does the body mistakenly appear to be Ātman due to ignorance.

महत्त्वे सर्ववस्तूनामणुत्वं ह्यतिदूरतः।
तद्वदात्मनि देहत्वं पश्यत्यज्ञानयोगतः ॥८०॥
mahattve sarvavastūnāmaṇutvaṁ hyatidūrataḥ,
tadvadātmani dehatvaṁ paśyatyajñānayogataḥ.

80. Just as all really large things appear to be very small owing to great distance, so does the body mistakenly appear to be Ātman due to ignorance.

सूक्ष्मत्वे सर्ववस्तूनां स्थूलत्वं चोपनेत्रतः।
तद्वदात्मनि देहत्वं पश्यत्यज्ञानयोगतः ॥८१॥
sūkṣamatve sarvavastūnāṁ sthūlatvaṁ chopanetrataḥ,
tadvadātmani dehatvaṁ paśyatyajñānayogataḥ.

81. Just as all very small objects appear large when viewed through lenses, the body mistakenly appears to be Ātman due to ignorance.

काचभूमौ जलत्वं वा जलभूमौ हि काचता।
तद्वदात्मनि देहत्वं पश्यत्यज्ञानयोगतः ॥८२॥
kāchabhūmau jalatvaṁ vā jalabhūmau hi kāchatā,
tadvadātmani dehatvaṁ paśyatyajñānayogataḥ.

82. Just as we might confuse the smooth surface of glass for a shimmering body of water and water for glass, so too does the body, clouded by ignorance, give the false impression of being the true Ātman.

यद्वदग्नौ मणित्वं हि मणौ वा वह्निता पुमान्।
तद्वदात्मनि देहत्वं पश्यत्यज्ञानयोगतः।।८३।।
yadvadagnau maṇitvaṁ hi maṇau vā vahnitā pumān,
tadvadātmani dehatvaṁ paśyatyajñānayogataḥ.

83. Just as a person perceives mistakenly a jewel in fire or fire in the jewel, so too does the body, clouded by ignorance, give the false impression of being the true Ātman.

अभ्रेषु सत्सु धावत्सु धावन्निव यथा शशी।
तद्वदात्मनि देहत्वं पश्यत्यज्ञानयोगतः ॥८४॥
abhreṣu satsu dhāvatsu dhāvanniva yathā śaśī,
tadvadātmani dehatvaṁ paśyatyajñānayogataḥ.

84. Just as when clouds move, the moon in moving clouds seems to be in motion; likewise, the body, clouded by ignorance, gives the false impression of being the true Ātman.

यथैव दिग्विपर्यासो मोहाद्भवति कस्यचित्।
तद्वदात्मनि देहत्वं पश्यत्यज्ञानयोगतः ॥८५॥
yathaiva digviparyāso mohādbhavati kasyachit,

tadvadātmani dehatvaṁ paśyatyajñānayogataḥ.

85. Just as a confused person loses their sense of direction, the body mistakenly appears to be the Ātman due to ignorance.

यथा शशी जले भाति चञ्चलत्वेन कस्यचित् ।
तद्वदात्मनि देहत्वं पश्यत्यज्ञानयोगतः ॥८६ ॥
yathā śaśī jale bhāti chañchalatvena kasyachit,
tadvadātmani dehatvaṁ paśyatyajñānayogataḥ.

86. Just as the moon appears unsteady when reflected in water, the body is mistakenly perceived as the Ātman due to ignorance.

एवमात्मनि नज्ञाते देहाध्यासो हि जायते ।
स एवात्मा परिज्ञातो लीयते च परात्मनि ॥८७ ॥
ēvamātmani najñāte dehādhyāso hi jāyate,
sa ēvātmā parijñāto līyate cha parātmani.

87. Through ignorance, the body is mistakenly identified as Ātman. When the true nature of Ātman is realized, the individual Ātman merges with the Supreme Ātman.

सर्वमात्मतया ज्ञातं जगत्स्थावरजङ्गमम् ।
अभावात्सर्वभावानां देहानां चात्मता कुतः ॥८८ ॥
sarvamātmatayā jñātaṁ jagatsthāvarajaṅgamam,
abhāvātsarvabhāvānāṁ dehānāṁ chātmatā kutaḥ.

88. When the entire universe, both movable and immovable, is understood to be created by Brahman, and in dissolution, the existence of everything else is absent, where is the justification to claim that the body is Ātman?

आत्मानं सततं जानन्कालं नय महामते ।
प्रारब्धमखिलं भुञ्जन्नोद्वेगं कर्तुमर्हसि ॥८९ ॥
ātmānaṁ satataṁ jānankālaṁ naya mahāmate,

prārabdhamakhilaṁ bhuñjannodvegaṁ kartumarhasi.

89. O enlightened one, always engage in self-realization while experiencing the results of prarābdha (past life karmas, which have begun to yield their fruits), you should not feel distressed.

उत्पन्नेऽप्यात्मविज्ञाने प्रारब्धं नैव मुञ्चति।
इति यच्छ्रूयते शास्त्रात्तन्निराक्रियतेऽधुना ॥९० ॥
utpanne'pyātmavijñāne prārabdhaṁ naiva muñchati,
iti yachchhrūyate śāstrāttannirākriyate'dhunā.

90. It is stated in some of the Śāstras that Prārabdha does not lose its influence on a person even after self-realization. This concept is now set aside.

तत्त्वज्ञानोदयादूर्ध्वं प्रारब्धं नैव विद्यते।
देहादीनामसत्यत्वाद्यथा स्वप्नः प्रबोधतः।।९१।।
tattvajñānodayādūrdhvaṁ prārabdhaṁ naiva vidyate,
dehādīnāmasatyatvādyathā svapnaḥ prabodhataḥ.

91. Self-realization occurs when prārabdha karmas are exhausted. Since both the body and the sense organs are perishable, they cease to exist after self-realization, similar to how a dream disappears upon waking.

It is important to note that a seeker cannot attain self-realization until they have experienced the consequences of their prārabdha karmas.

कर्म जन्मान्तरकृतं प्रारब्धमिति कीर्तितम्।
तत्तु जन्मान्तराभावात्पुंसो नैवास्ति कर्हिचित् ॥९२ ॥
karma janmāntarakṛtaṁ prārabdhamiti kīrtitam,
tattu janmāntarābhāvātpuṁso naivāsti karhichit.

92. That Karma which is done in a previous life is known as Prārabdha (which produces the present life). But such karma as becoming prārabdha cannot be performed

by a seeker because of the lack of body due to liberation.

स्वप्नदेहो यथाध्यस्तस्तथैवायं हि देहकः ॥
अध्यस्तस्य कुतो जन्म जन्माभावे स्थितिः कुतः ॥९३ ॥
svapnadeho yathādhyastastathaivāyaṁ hi dehakaḥ,
adhyastasya kuto janma janmābhāve sthitiḥ kutaḥ.

93. Just as the body in a dream is overlaid, this physical body is also a result of kārmika sanskāras (karmic impressions). A body that is only a superimposed form cannot take rebirth due to the lack of kārmika sanskāras. Without the possibility of rebirth, there is no place for the existence of prārabdha karmas (the karmas that have begun to manifest).

उपादानं प्रपञ्चस्य मृद्भाण्डस्येव कथ्यते ।
अज्ञानं चैव वेदान्तैस्तस्मिन्नष्टे क्व विश्वता ॥९४ ॥
upādānaṁ prapañchasya mṛdbhāṇḍasyeva kathyate,
ajñānaṁ chaiva vedāntaistasminnaṣṭe kva viśvatā.

94. The Vedāntins declare (ajñāna) sanskāras of prakṛti (material world) to be verily the material cause of the the body just as earth is of a pot. That ajñāna (prakṛti) being dessolved, where can the visible world subsist?

Note: Jñāna is the knowledge or sanskāras of the spiritual world, i.e. Ātman and Paramātman, and Ajñāna is the knowledge or sanskāras of the Material world. The ajñāna or the sanskāras of the material world are the cause of the embodiment of the soul.

यथा रज्जुं परित्यज्य सर्प गृह्णाति वै भ्रमात् ।
तद्वत्सत्यमविज्ञाय जगत्पश्यति मूढधीः ॥९५ ॥
yathā rajjuṁ parityajya sarpa gṛhṇāti vai bhramāt,
tadvatsatyamavijñāya jagatpaśyati mūḍhadhīḥ.

95. Just as a confused person perceives only the snake,

ignoring the rope, an ignorant person sees only the phenomenal world, unaware of the underlying reality.

रज्जुरूपे परिज्ञाते सर्पभ्रान्तिर्न तिष्ठति ।
अधिष्ठाने तथा ज्ञाते प्रपञ्चः शून्यतां व्रजेत् ॥९६ ॥
rajjurūpe parijñāte sarpabhrāntirna tiṣṭhati,
adhiṣṭhāne tathā jñāte prapañchaḥ śūnyatāṁ vrajet.

96. The real nature of the rope being known, the confusion of the snake no longer persists; so the [adhiṣṭhāna] inhabiting reality (soul) being realized, the body will appear insignificant.

देहस्यापि प्रपञ्चत्वात्प्रारब्धावस्थितिः कुतः ।
अज्ञानिजनबोधार्थं प्रारब्धं वक्ति वै श्रुतिः ॥९७ ॥
dehasyāpi prapañchatvātprārabdhāvasthitiḥ kutaḥ,
ajñānijanabodhārthaṁ prārabdhaṁ vakti vai śrutiḥ.

97. The body also being made of the material world, will perish after self-realization, how could Prārabdha exist? It is, therefore, for the understanding of the materialist person (involved in the material world) alone that the texts speak of Prārabdha.

Note: Karmas are performed when an ajñānī (materialist) is involved in the material world, so terms like prārabdha are applicable in the case of an ajñānī (materialist) and not in the case of a jñāni (spiritualist).

क्षीयन्ते चास्य कर्माणि तस्मिन्दृष्टे परावरे ।
बहुत्वं तन्निषेधार्थं श्रुत्या गीतं च वै स्फुटम् ॥९८ ॥
kṣīyante chāsya karmāṇi tasmindṛṣṭe parāvare,
bahutvaṁ tanniṣedhārthaṁ śrutyā gītaṁ cha vai sphuṭam.

98. "Man's all kārmika sanskāras are burnt when they realizes Brahman, which is both near and far." In this

statement, the use of the plural form in the Śruti emphasizes the negation of the existence of Prārabdha after realizing Brahman.

उच्यतेऽज्ञैर्बलाच्चैतत्तदानर्थद्वयागमः ।
वेदान्तमतहानं च यतो ज्ञानमिति श्रुतिः ॥९९ ॥
uchyate'jñairbalāchchaitattadānarthadvayāgamaḥ,
vedāntamatahānaṁ cha yato jñānamiti śrutiḥ.

99. If the [ajñaiḥ] materialists stubbornly adhere to material world sanskāras, they risk two major issues: accumulating karmas that lead to prārabdha (the fruits of past actions) and neglecting the path to self-realization. Therefore, one should accept only those texts that do not hinder the goal of attaining mokṣa (liberation).

त्रिपञ्चाङ्गान्यथो वक्ष्ये पूर्वोक्तस्यैव सिद्धये ।
तैश्च सर्वैः सदा कार्यं निदिध्यासनमेव तु ॥१०० ॥
tripañchāṅgānyatho vakṣaye pūrvoktasyaiva siddhaye,
taiścha sarvaiḥ sadā kāryaṁ nididhyāsanameva tu.

100. To achieve self-realisation, I will describe the three into five (fifteen steps) [nididhyāsana] for practicing profound meditation at all times.

नित्याभ्यासादृते प्राप्तिर्न भवेत्सच्चिदात्मनः ।
तस्माद्ब्रह्म निदिध्यासेज्जिज्ञासुः श्रेयसे चिरम् ॥१०१ ॥
nityābhyāsādṛte prāptirna bhavetsachchidātmanaḥ,
tasmādbrahma nididhyāsejjijñāsuḥ śreyase chiram.

101. To realize the eternal and immaterial Brahman, daily deep meditation is essential. Therefore, one who seeks Brahma-realization should engage in a prolonged meditation on Brahman to attain spiritual liberation (Mokṣa).

यमो हि नियमस्त्यागो मौनं देशश्च कालतः ।

आसनं मूलबन्धश्च देहसाम्यं च दृक्स्थितिः ।।१०२।।

yamo hi niyamastyāgo maunaṁ deśaścha kālataḥ, āsanaṁ mūlabandhaścha dehasāmyaṁ cha dṛksthitiḥ.

प्राणसंयमनं चैव प्रत्याहारश्च धारणा ।
आत्मध्यानं समाधिश्च प्रोक्तान्यङ्गानि वै क्रमात् ।।१०३।।

prāṇasaṁyamanaṁ chaiva pratyāhāraścha dhāraṇā, ātmadhyānaṁ samādhiścha proktānyaṅgāni vai kramāt.

The steps, in order, are described as follows:

1. Yama (social discipline)
2. Niyama (self-discipline).
3. Tyāga (sacrifice or renunciation)
4. Mauna (Silence)
5. Space of Brahman before creation (Solitude)
6. Kāla (Time)
7. Āsana (Posture)
8. Mūlabandha (Root lock)
9. Dehasāmya (Equipoise of body limbs)
10. Firmness of vision
11. Control of Prāṇa (Prāṇāyāma)
12. Pratyāhāra (withdrawal of mind)
13. Focus of mind
14. Ātmadhyāna (Meditation)
15. Samādhi

सर्वं ब्रह्मेति विज्ञानादिन्द्रियग्रामसंयमः ।
यमोऽयमिति संप्रोक्तोऽभ्यसनीयो मुहुर्मुहुः ।।१०४।।

sarvaṁ brahmeti vijñānādindriyagrāmasaṁyamaḥ,
yamo'yamiti saṁprokto'bhyasanīyo muhurmuhuḥ.

104. [vijñānāt] To realize [Brahmeti] Brahman [sarvam] everybody (indriyagrāmasañyamaḥ) should observe restrain of senses. By doing it we attain the perfection in yama (social discipline). This should be practiced again and again.

सजातीयप्रवाहश्च विजातीयतिरस्कृतिः।
नियमो हि परानन्दो नियमात्क्रियते बुधैः ॥१०५॥
sajātīyapravāhaścha vijātīyatiraskṛtiḥ,
niyamo hi parānando niyamātkriyate budhaiḥ.

105. The continuous flow of a single thought, excluding all others, is known as Niyama (self-discipline). Supreme bliss is achieved by those who wisely practice Niyama.

त्यागः प्रपञ्चरूपस्य चिदात्मत्वावलोकनात्।
त्यागो हि महतां पूज्यः सद्यो मोक्षमयो यतः ॥१०६॥
tyāgaḥ prapañcharūpasya chidātmatvāvalokanāt,
tyāgo hi mahatāṁ pūjyaḥ sadyo mokṣamayo yataḥ.

106. The renunciation of material objects, achieved through realizing the soul (Ātman), is the true form of renunciation sought by great seekers, as it leads to immediate liberation.

यतो वाचो निवर्तन्ते अप्राप्य मनसा सह।
यन्मौनं योगिभिर्गम्यं तद्भजेत्सर्वदा बुधः ॥१०७॥
yato vācho nivartante aprāpya manasā saha,
yanmaunaṁ yogibhirgamyaṁ tadbhajetsarvadā budhaḥ.

107. Silence, or Mauna, is the state that arises when the mind becomes separated from the organ of speech. Yogīs

maintain this silence, and thus the wise should practice it.

वाचो यस्मान्निवर्तन्ते तद्वक्तुं केन शक्यते।
प्रपञ्चो यदि वक्तव्यः सोऽपि शब्दविवर्जितः ॥१०८॥
vācho yasmānnivartante tadvaktuṁ kena śakyate,
prapañcho yadi vaktavyaḥ so'pi śabdavivarjitaḥ.

108. Who can describe that (Brahman) whose realization silences speech? If a seeker attempts to describe the phenomenal world at the stage of Brahma-realization, it too will be in a silent manner.

इति वा तद्भवेन्मौनं सतां सहजसंज्ञितम्।
गिरा मौनं तु बालानां प्रयुक्तं ब्रह्मवादिभिः ॥१०९॥
iti vā tadbhavenmaunaṁ satāṁ sahajasaṁjñitam,
girā maunaṁ tu bālānāṁ prayuktaṁ brahmavādibhiḥ.

109. Or we can say that the wise observe silence naturally, whereas the ignorant need to be directed to observe silence by restraining speech by the teachers of Brahman.

आदावन्ते च मध्ये च जनो यस्मिन्न विद्यते।
येनेदं सततं व्याप्तं स देशो विजनः स्मृतः ॥११०॥
ādāvante cha madhye cha jano yasminna vidyate,
yenedaṁ satataṁ vyāptaṁ sa deśo vijanaḥ smṛtaḥ.

110. That solitude is known as space of Brahman, wherein the universe does not exist in the beginning, end or middle, but is permeated by Brahman at all times.

कलनात्सर्वभूतानां ब्रह्मादीनां निमेषतः।
कालशब्देन निर्दिष्टो ह्यखण्डानन्द अद्वयः ॥१११॥
kalanātsarvabhūtānāṁ brahmādīnāṁ nimeṣataḥ,
kālaśabdena nirdiṣṭo hyakhaṇḍānanda advayaḥ.

111. Kāla is the measurement of time that ranges from Nimeṣa, which represents micro units of time, to the year

of Brāhma, equivalent to 4.32 billion years multiplied by 360, the largest macro unit of time. During creation, the indivisible and unparalleled Brahman is referred to as Kāla. In contrast, during dissolution, Brahman is known as Akāla.

सुखेनैव भवेद्यस्मिन्नजस्रं ब्रह्मचिन्तनम् ।
आसनं तद्विजानीयान्नेतरत्सुखनाशनम् । ।११२ । ।
sukhenaiva bhavedyasminnajasraṁ brahmachintanam,
āsanaṁ tadvijānīyānnetaratsukhanāśanam.

112. Āsana, or posture, is that which enables comfortable, constant meditation on Brahman, rather than an uncomfortable one.

सिद्धं यत्सर्वभूतादि विश्वाधिष्ठानमव्ययम् ।
यस्मिन्सिद्धाः समाविष्टास्तद्वै सिद्धासनं विदुः ॥११३ ॥
siddhaṁ yatsarvabhūtādi viśvādhiṣṭhānamavyayam,
yasminsiddhāḥ samāviṣṭāstadvai siddhāsanaṁ viduḥ.

113. Siddhāsana is a posture that aids in the realization of Brahman, who exists at the beginning of the universe's creation, inhabits the entire universe, and is imperishable. This posture was practiced by the Siddhas, the successful seekers of self-realization, on their path to realizing Brahman.

यन्मूलं सर्वभूतानां यन्मूलं चित्तबन्धनम् ।
मूलबन्धः सदा सेव्यो योगोऽसौ राजयोगिनाम् ॥११४ ॥
yanmūlaṁ sarvabhūtānāṁ yanmūlaṁ
chittabandhanam,
mūlabandhaḥ sadā sevyo yogo'sau rājayoginām.

114. The practice of Mūlabandha, or Root Lock, involves the intentional contraction of the pelvic floor muscles. This powerful technique not only facilitates the creation of life but also serves as a means to control and

focus the mind. Regular practice of Mūlabandha is essential, especially for those on the path of Rāja Yoga, as it enhances both physical vitality and mental discipline. Embrace this transformative practice to unlock your full potential.

अङ्गानां समतां विद्यात्समे ब्रह्मणि लीयते।
नो चेन्नैव समानत्वमृजुत्वं शुष्कवृक्षवत् ॥११५॥
aṅgānāṁ samatāṁ vidyātsame brahmaṇi līyate,
no chennaiva samānatvamṛjutvaṁ śuṣkavṛkṣavat.

115. Merging with Brahman leads to a balanced positioning of the limbs; otherwise, simply straightening the body like a lifeless tree does not create true balance.

दृष्टिं ज्ञानमयीं कृत्वा पश्येद्ब्रह्ममयं जगत्।
सा दृष्टिः परमोदारा न नासाग्रावलोकनी।।११६।।
dṛṣṭiṁ jñānamayīṁ kṛtvā paśyedbrahmamayaṁ jagat,
sā dṛṣṭiḥ paramodārā na nāsāgrāvalokanī.

116. Transforming ordinary vision into a profound understanding requires perceiving the world infused with Brahman. This enlightened perspective is the highest form of vision, unlike merely focusing on the tip of one's nose.

द्रष्टृदर्शनदृश्यानां विरामो यत्र वा भवेत्।
दृष्टिस्तत्रैव कर्तव्या न नासाग्रावलोकनी ॥११७॥
draṣṭṛdarśanadṛśyānāṁ virāmo yatra vā bhavet,
dṛṣṭistatraiva kartavyā na nāsāgrāvalokanī.

117. The true nature of vision occurs when the seer, sight, and what is seen become one, transcending a narrow focus on the tip of nose.

चित्तादिसर्वभावेषु ब्रह्मत्वेनैव भावनात्।
निरोधः सर्ववृत्तीनां प्राणायामः स उच्यते ॥११८॥
chittādisarvabhāveṣu brahmatvenaiva bhāvanāt,

nirodhaḥ sarvavṛttīnāṁ prāṇāyāmaḥ sa uchyate.

118. Concentrating on Brahman during all mental activities is known as withdrawing the mind from the external world. This practice is also referred to as Prāṇāyāma.

निषेधनं प्रपञ्चस्य रेचकाख्यः समीरणः ।
ब्रह्मैवास्मीति या वृत्तिः पूरको वायुरीरितः ॥११९ ॥
niṣedhanaṁ prapañchasya rechakākhyaḥ samīraṇaḥ,
brahmaivāsmīti yā vṛttiḥ pūrako vāyurīritaḥ.

119. Rechaka (exhalation) aids in withdrawing the mind from the material world, while Pūraka (inhalation) assists in realizing one's true nature as the soul rather than the body.

ततस्तद्वृत्तिनैश्चल्यं कुम्भकः प्राणसंयमः ।
अयं चापि प्रबुद्धानामज्ञानां घ्राणपीडनम् ॥१२० ॥
tatastadvṛttinaiśchalyaṁ kumbhakaḥ prāṇasaṁyamaḥ,
ayaṁ chāpi prabuddhānāmajñānāṁ ghrāṇapīḍanam.

120. Kumbhaka, or breath retention, contributes to a stable mind. This is the true essence of Prāṇāyāma for the enlightened, while the uninformed merely press their noses.

विषयेष्वात्मतां दृष्ट्वा मनसश्चिति मज्जनम् ।
प्रत्याहारः स विज्ञेयोऽभ्यसनीयो मुमुक्षुभिः ॥१२१ ॥
viṣayeṣvātmatāṁ dṛṣṭvā manasaśchiti majjanam,
pratyāhāraḥ sa vijñeyo'bhyasanīyo mumukṣubhiḥ.

121. When the soul becomes the object of the sense organs and the mind absorbs in the soul, it is known as Pratyāhāra, which should be practiced by seekers of liberation.

यत्र यत्र मनो याति ब्रह्मणस्तत्र दर्शनात् ।

मनसो धारणायैव धारणा सा परा मता ॥१२२ ॥

yatra yatra mano yāti brahmaṇastatra darśanāt,
manaso dhāraṇāyaiva dhāraṇā sā parā matā.

122. If Brahman becomes the focus of the mind wherever it goes, this is called Dhāraṇā because of the focused mind.

ब्रह्मैवास्मीति सद्वृत्त्या निरालम्बतया स्थितिः ।
ध्यानशब्देन विख्याता परमानन्ददायिनी ॥१२३ ॥

brahmaivāsmīti sadvṛttyā nirālambatayā sthitiḥ,
dhyānaśabdena vikhyātā paramānandadāyinī.

123. When a seeker realizes his/her true nature as 'I am the soul,' independent of the body and senses, this state is known as dhyāna and produces supreme bliss.

निर्विकारतया वृत्त्या ब्रह्माकारतया पुनः ।
वृत्तिविस्मरणं सम्यक्समाधिर्ज्ञानसंज्ञकः ॥१२४ ॥

nirvikāratayā vṛttyā brahmākāratayā punaḥ,
vṛttivismaraṇaṁ samyaksamādhirjñānasaṁjñakaḥ.

124. When the mind is free of all sanskāras and merges with the soul by letting go of all vṛttis (modes), this state is known as samādhi, which is characterized by self-realization.

एवं चाकृत्रिमानन्दं तावत्साधु समभ्यसेत् ।
वश्यो यावत्क्षणात्पुंसः प्रयुक्तः स भवेत्स्वयम् ॥१२५ ॥

ēvaṁ chākṛtrimānandaṁ tāvatsādhu samabhyaset,
vaśyo yāvatkṣaṇātpuṁsaḥ prayuktaḥ sa bhevatsvayam.

125. The seeker should [sādhu samabhyaset] diligently practice the samādhi that produces [akṛtrim+ānandam] natural bliss [vaśyaḥ yāvat kṣaṇāt punsaḥ] until they attain self-realization, thus [prayuktaḥ sa bhavet svayam] identifying their true nature.

ततः साधननिर्मुक्तः सिद्धो भवति योगिराट् ।
तत्स्वरूपं न चैकस्य विषयो मनसो गिराम् ॥१२६ ॥
tataḥ sādhananirmuktaḥ siddho bhavati yogirāṭ,
tatsvarūpaṁ na chaikasya viṣayo manaso girām.

126. Then he, the best among Yogīs having attained to perfection, becomes free from all practices. The real nature of such a seeker never becomes an object of the mind or speech.

समाधौ क्रियमाणे तु विघ्ना आयान्ति वै बलात् ।
अनुसंधानराहित्यमालस्यं भोगलालसम् ॥१२७ ॥
लयस्तमश्च विक्षेपो रसास्वादश्च शून्यता ।
एवं यद्विघ्नबाहुल्यं त्याज्यं ब्रह्मविदा शनैः ॥१२८ ॥
samādhau kriyamāṇe tu vighnā āyānti vai balāt,
anusaṁdhānarāhityamālasyaṁ bhogalālasam.
layastamaścha vikṣepo rasāsvādaścha śūnyatā,
ēvaṁ yadvighnabāhulyaṁ tyājyaṁ brahmavidā śanaiḥ.

127. – 128. While practicing Samādhi, various obstacles are likely to arise, including a lack of inquiry, idleness, desires for sensory pleasures, sleepiness, dullness, distraction, fleeting moments of joy, and feelings of emptiness. Anyone seeking Brahman should gradually work to overcome these numerous barriers.

भाववृत्त्या हि भावत्वं शून्यवृत्त्या हि शून्यता ।
ब्रह्मवृत्त्या हि पूर्णत्वं तथा पूर्णत्वमभ्यसेत् ॥१२९ ॥
bhāvavṛttyā hi bhāvatvaṁ śūnyavṛttyā hi śūnyatā,
brahmavṛttyā hi pūrṇatvaṁ tathā pūrṇatvamabhyaset.

129. When contemplating an object, the mind identifies with it, and when considering a void, it becomes blank. However, by thinking of the soul, one [pūrṇatvam] can achieve self-realization. Therefore, one should consistently [abhyaset] practice [pūrṇatvam] self-

realization.

ये हि वृत्तिं जहत्येनां ब्रह्माख्यां पावनीं पराम्।
वृथैव ते तु जीवन्ति पशुभिश्च समा नराः ॥१३०॥
ye hi vṛttiṁ jahatyenāṁ brahmākhyāṁ pāvanīṁ parām,
vṛthaiva te tu jīvanti paśubhiścha samā narāḥ.

130. Those who neglect to focus their minds on the purifying thought of Brahman live meaningless lives and are no better than animals.

ये हि वृत्तिं विजानन्ति ये ज्ञात्वा वर्धयन्त्यपि।
ते वै सत्पुरुषा धन्या वन्द्यास्ते भुवनत्रये ॥१३१॥
ye hi vṛttiṁ vijānanti ye jñātvā vardhayantyapi,
te vai satpuruṣā dhanyā vandyāste bhuvanatraye.

131. Truly blessed are the virtuous individuals who concentrate their minds on Brahman and continually strive to deepen their understanding. They are held in high regard everywhere.

येषां वृत्तिः समावृद्धा परिपक्वा च सा पुनः।
ते वै सद्ब्रह्मतां प्राप्ता नेतरे शब्दवादिनः ॥१३२॥
yeṣāṁ vṛttiḥ samāvṛddhā paripakvā cha sā punaḥ,
te vai sadbrahmatāṁ prāptā netare śabdavādinaḥ.

132. Only those whose minds are focused on Brahman and who grow into maturity attain the state of ever-existent Brahman (mokṣa); others, merely dealing with words, do not.

कुशला ब्रह्मवार्तायां वृत्तिहीनाः सुरागिणः।
तेऽप्यज्ञानितमा नूनं पुनरायान्ति यान्ति च ॥१३३॥
kuśalā brahmavārtāyāṁ vṛttihīnāḥ surāgiṇaḥ,
te'pyajñānitamā nūnaṁ punarāyānti yānti cha.

133. Those who are experts in discussing Brahman, yet lack focus on him and are overly attached to worldly

pleasures, are the most ignorant, being born and dying repeatedly.

निमेषार्धं न तिष्ठन्ति वृत्तिं ब्रह्ममयीं विना।
यथा तिष्ठन्ति ब्रह्माद्याः सनकाद्याः शुकादयः ॥१३४॥
nimeṣārdhaṁ na tiṣṭhanti vṛttiṁ brahmamayīṁ vinā,
yathā tiṣṭhanti brahmādyāḥ sanakādyāḥ śukādayaḥ.

134. The seekers of Brahman are unwavering in their devotion, holding the thought of Brahman in their minds at every moment. They are driven by the same relentless pursuit as revered figures like Brahmā, Sanaka, Śuka, and others.

कार्ये कारणतायाता कारणे न हि कार्यता।
कारणत्वं स्वतो गच्छेत्कार्याभावे विचारतः ॥१३५॥
kārye kāraṇatāyātā kāraṇe na hi kāryatā,
kāraṇatvaṁ svato gachchhetkāryābhāve vichārataḥ.

135. The effect has the qualities of the material cause, but the material cause does not have the qualities of the effect; therefore, when the absence of the effect is considered, the material cause also disappears. When the absence of a visible world is considered, its material cause (prakṛti) won't come into sight.

अथ शुद्धं भवेद्वस्तु यद्वै वाचामगोचरः।
द्रष्टव्यं मृद्धटेनैव दृष्टान्तेन पुनः पुनः ॥१३६॥
atha śuddhaṁ bhavedvastu yadvai vāchāmagocharaḥ,
draṣṭavyaṁ mṛddhaṭenaiva dṛṣṭāntena punaḥ punaḥ.

136. However, the pure reality (Brahman), which is the efficient cause of the universe, exists beyond the description of the speech. This concept should be understood repeatedly through the analogy of the earth and the pot. For instance, when the pot is absent, the material cause of the pot—the earth—ceases to be the

subject of thought. However, the potter, who is the efficient cause, remains.

अनेनैव प्रकारेण वृत्तिर्ब्रह्मात्मिका भवेत्।
उदेति शुद्धचित्तानां वृत्तिज्ञानं ततः परम् ॥१३७॥
anenaiva prakāreṇa vṛttirbrahmātmikā bhavet,
udeti śuddhachittānāṁ vṛttijñānaṁ tataḥ param.

137. Similarly, the mind's focus turns towards Brahman. This tendency of mental concentration on Brahman first emerges in pure-hearted individuals, leading to self-realization.

कारणं व्यतिरेकेण पुमानादौ विलोकयेत्।
अन्वयेन पुनस्तद्धि कार्ये नित्यं प्रपश्यति ॥१३८॥
kāraṇaṁ vyatirekeṇa pumānādau vilokayet,
anvayena punastaddhi kārye nityaṁ prapaśyati.

138. One should first identify the cause by ruling out dissimilar attributes and gathering the similar attributes inherent in the effect.

कार्ये हि कारणं पश्येत्पश्चात्कार्यं विसर्जयेत्।
कारणत्वं स्वतो नश्येदवशिष्टं भवेन्मुनिः ॥१३९॥
kārye hi kāraṇaṁ paśyetpaśchātkāryaṁ visarjayet,
kāraṇatvaṁ svato naśyedavaśiṣṭaṁ bhavenmuniḥ.

139. One should identify the cause of an effect. Once the cause is identified, the effect can be dismissed so that the cause itself will be eliminated. What remains is the seeker himself.

Note: The author presents a method of self-realization. To begin, one should identify the true cause of the body. The karmic sanskaras are responsible for the formation of the body. Once this understanding is established, the seeker should eliminate all actions that create sanskaras leading to the formation of the body. By doing so, the body will be eliminated and only the soul will remain, called self-realization.

भावितं तीव्रवेगेण वस्तु यन्निश्चयात्मना।
पुमांस्तद्धि भवेच्छीघ्रं ज्ञेयं भ्रमरकीटवत् ॥१४०॥
bhāvitaṁ tīvravegeṇa vastu yanniśchayātmanā,
pumāṁstaddhi bhavechchhīghraṁ jñeyaṁ bhramarakīṭavat.

140. If something is meditated with a determined mind, the meditator becomes one with that very thing. This may be understood from the illustration of the wasp and the worm, where a wasp brought a worm in its hole, and the worm out of fear constantly thought of it till it transformed into a wasp itself. Thus a seeker who constantly meditates on Brahman becomes one with Brahman (attains mokṣa).

अदृश्यं भावरूपं च सर्वमेतच्चिदात्मकम्।
सावधानतया नित्यं स्वात्मानं भावयेद्बुधः ॥१४१॥
adṛśyaṁ bhāvarūpaṁ cha sarvametachchidātmakam,
sāvadhānatayā nityaṁ svātmānaṁ bhāvayedbudhaḥ.

141. Therefore, the wise should always meditate carefully on the invisible, abstract and immaterial Brahman.

दृश्यं ह्यदृश्यतां नीत्वा ब्रह्माकारेण चिन्तयेत्।
विद्वान्नित्यसुखे तिष्ठेद्धिया चिद्रसपूर्णया।।१४२।।
dṛśyaṁ hyadṛśyatāṁ nītvā brahmākāreṇa chintayet,
vidvānnityasukhe tiṣṭheddhiyā chidrasapūrṇayā.

142. By avoiding attention from the visible to the invisible, the wise should contemplate the Brahman alone. The yogī will dwell in eternal bliss, with a mind filled with the joy of self-realization.

एभिरङ्गैः समायुक्तो राजयोग उदाहृतः ।
किंचित्पक्वकषायाणां हठयोगेन संयुतः ॥१४३ ॥
ēbhiraṅgaiḥ samāyukto rājayoga udāhṛtaḥ,
kiṁchitpakvakaṣāyāṇāṁ haṭhayogena saṁyutaḥ.

143. Thus, the Rāja-Yoga consisted of the aforementioned steps has been described. This can be combined with Haṭha-Yoga for those whose worldly desires are somewhat dimnished.

परिपक्वं मनो येषां केवलोऽयं च सिद्धिदः ।
गुरुदैवतभक्तानां सर्वेषां सुलभो जवात् ॥१४४ ॥
paripakvaṁ mano yeṣāṁ kevalo'yaṁ cha siddhidaḥ,
gurudaivatabhaktānāṁ sarveṣāṁ sulabho javāt.

144. For those whose minds are completely purified, this Rāja-Yoga is the sole path to perfection. This perfection is also swiftly accessible to those who are devoted to the teacher and the targeted Devatā, Brahman.

इति श्रीमत्परमहंसपरिव्राजकाचार्यस्य श्रीगोविन्दभगवत्पूज्यपादशिष्यस्य
श्रीमच्छंकरभगवतः कृतौ अपरोक्षानुभूतिः समाप्ता ॥
iti śrīmatparamahaṁsaparivrājakāchāryasya
Śrīgovindabhagavatpūjyapādaśiṣyasya
Śrīmachchhaṅkarabhagavataḥ kṛtau
aparokṣānubhūtiḥ samāptā ॥

Thus, ends here the 'Direct Self Realization' authored by Śrimat Śaṅkarāchārya, the disciple of Śri Govind Āchārya.